William Harrison Ainsworth

Merry England

Vol. 2

William Harrison Ainsworth

Merry England
Vol. 2

ISBN/EAN: 9783337778743

Printed in Europe, USA, Canada, Australia, Japan

Cover: Foto ©Thomas Meinert / pixelio.de

More available books at **www.hansebooks.com**

MERRY ENGLAND:

OR,

NOBLES AND SERFS.

BY

WILLIAM HARRISON AINSWORTH,

AUTHOR OF
"THE TOWER OF LONDON," "BOSCOBEL," ETC.

"In order that gentlemen and others may take example and correct wicked rebels, I will most amply detail how this business was conducted."
FROISSART.

IN THREE VOLUMES.
VOL. II.

LONDON:
TINSLEY BROTHERS, 8, CATHERINE STREET, STRAND.
1874.

[*Right of Translation reserved by the Author.*]

CONTENTS

OF

THE SECOND VOLUME.

BOOK I.—*continued.*

THE INSURRECTION.

		PAGE
XXXV.	HOW SAINT THOMAS'S SHRINE WAS DEFENDED BY FRIAR NOSROCK	3
XXXVI.	CONRAD BASSET AND CATHERINE DE COURCY	12
XXXVII.	FRIDESWIDE	22
XXXVIII.	THE DEPARTURE OF THE REBELS FROM CANTERBURY	26

BOOK II.

THE YOUNG KING.

I.	EDITHA IS APPOINTED ONE OF THE PRINCESS'S ATTENDANTS	35
II.	ELTHAM PALACE	42
III.	RICHARD OF BORDEAUX	52
IV.	THE MEETING BETWEEN THE YOUNG KING AND EDITHA	64
V.	SIR EUSTACE DE VALLETORT OBTAINS SOME INFORMATION FROM THE PRINCESS	68
VI.	SIR SIMON BURLEY	76
VII.	SIR WILLIAM WALWORTH AND SIR JOHN PHILPOT	86
VIII.	THE ARCHBISHOP OF CANTERBURY AND THE LORD OF ST. JOHN'S	95

		PAGE
IX.	THE BARON DE VERTAIN AND SIR JOHN PHILPOT PROPOSE TO ATTACK THE REBELS	107
X.	THE LIEUTENANT OF THE TOWER	115
XI.	SIR EUSTACE DE VALLETORT MAKES A DISCLOSURE TO EDITHA	124
XII.	HOW SIR JOHN HOLLAND RETURNED FROM THE EXPEDITION	136
XIII.	SIR JOHN HOLLAND'S NARRATIVE	145
XIV.	CONRAD BASSET DEMANDS THAT SIR JOHN HOLLAND SHALL BE DELIVERED UP	152
XV.	THE SUBTERRANEAN PASSAGE	160
XVI.	HOW THE PRINCESS ARRIVED AT THE TOWER	173
XVII.	HOW SIR SIMON BURLEY, THE BARON DE GOMMEGINES, AND THE LORD MAYOR SET OUT TO SUCCOUR THE BESIEGED AT ELTHAM PALACE	
XVIII.	WHAT BEFEL SIR OSBERT MONTACUTE ON HIS RETURN THROUGH THE SUBTERRANEAN PASSAGE	192
XIX.	HOW ELTHAM PALACE WAS VALIANTLY DEFENDED BY SIR JOHN PHILPOT	200
XX.	HOW THE PALACE WAS DELIVERED	211

BOOK III.

BLACKHEATH.

I.	THE SIEGE OF ROCHESTER CASTLE	221
II.	WAT TYLER REVISITS DARTFORD	231
III.	THE HERMIT'S WARNING	241
IV.	THE OUTLAW ACCEPTS THE COMMAND OF THE ESSEX BATTALION	247

BOOK I.—*continued.*

THE INSURRECTION.

MERRY ENGLAND;

OR,

NOBLES AND SERFS.

XXXV.

HOW SAINT THOMAS'S SHRINE WAS DEFENDED BY FRIAR NOSROCK.

HILE most of the household concealed themselves in the crypts of the cathedral, Sir John Holland and the young nobles, by the advice of the unfortunate seneschal, proceeded to Trinity Chapel, where they found Friar Nosrock, who took them to the watching-chamber.

There they remained during the rest of the day, fully expecting that the rebels would come in quest of them; but, to their surprise, they were undisturbed. As yet, they were ignorant of Siward's fate.

When night came on, they resolved to quit their asylum, though Friar Nosrock represented to them that they would run the greatest risk in venturing forth into the city.

"Should you fall into the hands of the rebels, you will certainly be put to death," he said; "and you will find it almost impossible to leave the city, since the gates are guarded, and all other outlets stopped. The Abbot of St. Vincent will give you an asylum, if he can, and so will the Prior of St. Augustine's; but should you be driven to extremity, and compelled to return hither, come back in the guise of pilgrims. I myself will be on the watch, and will take care you shall be admitted by the south porch."

He then led them out by a postern, and

returned to Trinity Chapel, where he found the Archbishop's household assembled. As these persons had been all this time in the crypts, they had not heard what had befallen Siward; but they augured ill since he had not reappeared.

After some consultation, it was decided that half a dozen of the men should remain with Friar Nosrock to keep watch throughout the night; the rest, including the female servants, quitted the cathedral by the postern.

We have already stated that certain of the Dartford insurgents had secured the large dormitory at the "Chequers," and had, moreover, ordered a good supper to be provided for a hundred persons.

At the appointed hour a plentiful repast was set before these unwelcome guests, and while they were discussing it, it occurred to Mark Cleaver, Liripipe, and some others, that they might contrive to possess themselves of the treasures of Becket's shrine.

Communicated in an undertone to the whole party, the plan met with general approval, and it was resolved that the attempt should be made that very night. Should it succeed, they would all be enriched. But it would be necessary to enter the cathedral by stratagem, since Wat Tyler had prohibited any attempt to break into it by force for purposes of plunder, on pain of death.

After some deliberation, they resolved to seek admittance as pilgrims, the notion being suggested to them by the fact that there were a great number of devotees staying at the "Chequers," who desired to offer prayers at the shrine at night.

Accordingly, having arrayed themselves as they best could, in imitation of these pilgrims, the whole party, having previously assembled in the courtyard of the inn, set out without noise, and on reaching the south porch of the cathedral, knocked against the great door.

Now it chanced that Friar Nosrock, who fully expected the return of Sir John Holland and the young nobles, was waiting near the door at the time, and when he heard that those who knocked were pilgrims, he imprudently opened the wicket.

Very few had entered before he discovered his mistake, but it was then too late.

Breaking from the foremost, who tried to seize him, he ran as swiftly as he could along the aisle, and through the south transept of St. Thomas's Chapel, where he suddenly disappeared from his pursuers, who were close at his heels.

In another minute, all the plunderers, with the exception of two or three, who had been left at the south porch to keep watch, arrived at the foot of the steps leading to the shrine.

A lamp burning above the altar dimly illumined the chapel, but afforded sufficient light for their sacrilegious purpose.

Several clambered over the gilt rails surrounding the sacred spot, and proceeded to lift up the heavy wooden canopy covering the shrine.

While thus employed, they were suddenly interrupted in their task by an occurrence that seemed as if Saint Thomas himself had interfered to prevent the threatened desecration of his shrine.

A fierce growling was heard, and then came the fearful rush of a number of savage hounds towards those collected on the steps.

Terrible outcries followed from those who imagined they were attacked by demons in shape of dogs, and now fled, yelling, in every direction.

These suffered severely from the sharp fangs of their pursuers, but those near the shrine fared the worst.

Caught as in a trap by their ferocious assailants, who leaped over the rails and sprang at their throats, bearing them to the ground, they had to fight for their lives, and the vaulted roof of the chapel rang with their cries.

A witness of this frightful scene, Friar Nosrock felt little compassion for the miserable wretches.

On the contrary, he called out to them, in a mocking voice—

"Soh! you would plunder the shrine of holy St. Thomas, eh? You thought it an easy task, doubtless—but you now find we can prevent your villany!"

"Save us!" cried Mark Cleaver, who was lying prostrate on the pavement, with a huge hound standing over him. "Save us!

or we shall be torn in pieces by these infernal hounds—if indeed they be hounds, and not fiends!"

"Have pity upon us, good brother, and call them off!" implored Liripipe, who had shrunk into a corner, and was endeavouring to keep one of his fierce assailants at bay. "Let us out of this cage, and we will depart at once!"

"You deserve the worst punishment that can befall you!" cried Friar Nosrock.

"Holy St. Thomas, have mercy upon us!" cried Curthose, who was in as sore distress as the others. "We heartily repent what we have done! Instead of robbing the shrine, we will add to its riches."

"Have mercy upon us, holy St. Thomas!" cried all the sufferers.

"Since you call upon the good saint for aid, it will not be refused you," said the friar, somewhat relenting.

And as he spoke, he opened a gate in the rails, and called off the hounds.

"Depart instantly!" he said. "If any of you be found in the cathedral five minutes hence, no further pity shall be shown you!"

Glad to escape on such terms, the villains came forth; and though they were all in a most deplorable condition, they contrived in a short time to reach the south porch.

Friar Nosrock was close at their heels with his hounds, and carefully barred the door as the last of them went out.

Shortly afterwards, the friar was joined by such of the Archbishop's household as had remained in the cathedral.

Assisted by them, and attended by his hounds, he made a strict investigation of the aisles, the nave, the transepts, and the choir.

No one was found.

Nevertheless, watch was kept by the party throughout the night.

XXXVI.

CONRAD BASSET AND CATHERINE DE COURCY.

THAT night, Canterbury was completely in the power of the insurgents.

The six gates were strictly guarded, so that no one could leave the city, or enter it, without permission from the rebel leaders.

Every precaution was taken to prevent the escape of Sir John Holland and the young nobles, and Wat Tyler persuaded himself he should have them in his hands on the morrow; in which case he had fully resolved to put Sir John to death.

But he was baulked in his vindictive design. After quitting the cathedral, Sir John and his companions had repaired to the

Monastery of St. Augustine; where they were well received by the Abbot, and carefully concealed by him. Though strict search was made for them, their retreat was not discovered.

The three insurgent leaders fixed their quarters in the Palace, and remained there during their stay in the city.

Their time was chiefly spent in the great hall, where they held a sort of Court.

Ordering the Mayor and aldermen to appear before them, they compelled them, on pain of death, to take the oath of fidelity to the league.

Since their arrival at Canterbury, the force under the command of the rebel leaders had enormously increased, and it now seemed certain that five hundred of the citizens would march with them to London.

Under these circumstances, it became necessary to appoint officers; and the appointments were made by Wat Tyler and the Outlaw, who selected those whom they thought could be best depended upon.

A fierce wild set they were, most of them belonging to the lowest orders of the people. Among the few of a higher class, was Conrad Basset, the brewer's son.

This young man had recommended himself to the rebel leaders by a hatred of the nobles, almost equalling their own in intensity.

This animosity, however, did not arise from sympathy with the oppressed peasantry, but from the ignominious manner in which he had been treated by Sir Lionel de Courcy, of whose beautiful daughter, Catherine, he had become passionately enamoured.

Conrad Basset, who was handsomer than many of the high-born youths she had seen, had attracted the fair Catherine de Courcy's attention; and after a few words had been exchanged between them at the cathedral and elsewhere, they met one night in the garden of her father's mansion in Canterbury.

This secret interview was their first and last. They were surprised by Sir Lionel, who came suddenly upon them with a party of servants, and having sent Catherine into the house, turned to her lover, who had been seized by a couple of servants, and after applying to him every scornful epithet that fury could suggest, he said—

"Thy father, Richard Basset, was my vassal; and when I set him free, I little thought his son would have the presumption to address my daughter in language of love. But I will punish thee as I would a disobedient serf."

With this he took a staff from one of his valets, and struck the young man several hard blows with it, calling out—

"This will teach thee, thou low-born knave, to aspire to the daughter of a noble!"

Held fast by two powerful men, Conrad could offer no resistance to this usage, and he was cast out at the gate.

From that moment he thought only of revenge.

He still loved Catherine de Courcy passionately as ever, but he could not forgive her father for the degrading outrage he had inflicted upon him.

Nay, more; his vindictive feeling towards the one proud noble who had injured him extended to all his class, and when he heard of the insurrectionary league of the peasants, the object of which was to exterminate their lordly oppressors, he immediately joined it.

At length a full revenge seemed in his grasp.

When the insurgents entered Canterbury, Sir Lionel de Courcy—unfortunately for himself—chanced to be at home. But as he resided in a large and strongly-built mansion, and had a great number of armed retainers, he did not deem himself in danger.

But Conrad had determined to attack his house, and make him prisoner, and mentioned his design to the two rebel leaders, who approved of it.

It was fixed that the assault should take place on the morrow, and some preparations were made for it, under Conrad's personal direction.

That night two damsels, whose features were concealed by their hoods, sought a private interview with the young rebel captain.

It was granted; and when the damsels had removed their disguise, one of them proved to be Catherine de Courcy, and the other her handmaiden, Gertrude.

Catherine had never appeared so beautiful before, and Conrad's passion revived as he gazed at her.

"You must have expected me here tonight, Conrad," she said; "and you will guess that my errand is to beg my father's life. I know that if he should fall into your hands you will slay him——"

"Your father can expect no mercy from me," interrupted Conrad, fiercely.

"I will not believe you can be so cruel, Conrad," she rejoined. "If you kill my father, you will kill me."

"He has dishonoured me. Nothing but his blood can wash out the disgrace. Sir Lionel has made me what I am; and all the crimes I may commit will lie at his door."

"Oh, Conrad!" she exclaimed; "it is not too late to turn back. You are not meant to be the associate of rebels; your nature is loyal and true. Return to your allegiance to the King, and all will yet be well."

"I have joined this league, and am bound by oath to be faithful to it," he replied.

"You can easily be absolved from such an oath," she said. "Save my father, and I will answer for his gratitude."

"As well might you seek to wrest his prey from the tiger, as ask me to part with mine!" cried Conrad.

"Then farewell for ever!" she said. "You will rue your conduct when you see me stretched lifeless at your feet!"

A brief pause ensued, during which it was evident that a great struggle was going on in Conrad's breast.

In the hope of a change in his determination, Catherine stayed.

"You have conquered," he said at length.

"For your sake, Catherine, I will spare your father."

"Now I recognise you as a Conrad I loved!" she cried, springing towards him. "You will fly with us?" she added, gazing anxiously into his face; "you will abandon these dreadful rebels?"

"I cannot," he rejoined, firmly. "Not even you, Catherine, can induce me to break my plighted word."

She forbore to urge him further, and they parted.

Next morning Sir Lionel de Courcy's mansion, which was situated on the eastern side of the city, between the priories of St. John and St. Gregory, was attacked by a large body of the insurgents, and speedily taken, since no defence was made.

Sir Lionel, his daughter, and his entire household were gone.

Their flight had been secretly aided by Conrad and his followers.

The insurgents were greatly disappointed, for they meant to behead the knight; but they consoled themselves by plundering his mansion.

XXXVII.

FRIDESWIDE.

THE insurgents' last day in Canterbury was spent in feasting and carousing, and in plundering the Abbey of St. Vincent, and two or three smaller religious houses; but no further attempt was made upon the treasures of the cathedral.

The leaders continued to occupy the Archbishop's palace, where they held their councils and issued their decrees.

By this time such numbers had flocked to their standard that the city was quite full, and the monasteries and religious houses were invaded.

Five hundred citizens of Canterbury had

enrolled themselves in the revolutionary army, and signified their intention of accompanying them in their march to London.

To the command of this division, which was far better accoutred than the others, Conrad Basset was appointed.

When the grand muster of the army was made before Wat Tyler and the Outlaw, a young woman, of gigantic size, and strongly proportioned, presented herself, and desired to accompany the host.

The two leaders regarded her with wonder. Though her frame was large, it was well-proportioned, and her features, though masculine, were not coarse in expression; nor could she be termed ill-looking.

She gave her name as Frideswide, and described herself as the daughter of Maurice Balsam, the miller of Fordwich.

In age, Frideswide was not more than three-and-twenty.

Though the two rebel leaders had resolved to allow no woman to accompany the host, they were so much struck by this Amazon's appearance that they felt inclined to make an exception in her favour.

While they were conferring together, Frideswide said, "I do not care to boast, but there is no man in Kent, be he whom he may, who can draw a stronger bow than I can, or lift heavier weight. Give me a quarter-staff, and you shall see what I can do!"

And, her request being complied with, she added, "Now let any man strike me, if he can!"

On this there was a general laugh among the assemblage, but no one accepted the challenge.

However, when she told them they were afraid of her, a sturdy fellow stepped forward, brandishing a staff, and bade her look to herself.

Whether he was in jest or earnest matters not, but he quickly got a hard crack on the pate that stretched him on the ground, amid the laughter and cheers of the beholders.

"Now let another come on!" exclaimed Frideswide; "I am ready for twenty more!"

But no one ventured to attack her.

After this proof of her strength and skill, the insurgent leaders decided that Frideswide should be allowed to accompany the army, and she was placed with the Canterbury men, under the command of Conrad Basset.

XXXVIII.

THE DEPARTURE OF THE REBELS FROM CANTERBURY.

WHEN the host issued forth from the west gate it really presented an extraordinary spectacle, and such as had never before been witnessed in England.

Five hundred citizens of Canterbury, as we have already stated, had volunteered to accompany the march to London; but still the majority of the host was composed of peasantry supplied by the different Kentish villages.

Armed for the most part with pikes, scythes, and flails, and wearing their ordinary habiliments, they presented a singularly wild appearance.

An attempt was made to keep them together, and compel them to march in companies, but this was found impracticable.

The citizens of Canterbury were far better armed and accoutred, and carried a banner and pennons.

Trumpets were sounded, and drums beaten, as the leaders rode forth from the west gate, followed by this strange and disorderly host; and so vast were the numbers, that much delay occurred before all came forth.

The leaders, however, would not proceed on the march till the entire force was collected on the plain outside the city.

When all the stragglers had come up, John Ball took his mule to the top of a mound, and from his elevated position preached a sermon to the vast assemblage, taking for his text this couplet of his own composition :—

> "When Adam delved and Eve span,
> Who was then the gentleman?"

"Who, indeed?" he demanded in a loud, mocking voice. "Not the father of the human race. I tell you, my brethren," he continued, increasing in fervour as he went on, "that by nature all men were born equal, and that there ought to be no ranks, no distinctions. By nature all men are free, and bondage and servitude, which were never designed by heaven, but have been invented by our wicked oppressors, ought to be abolished. Heaven has, at last, given you the means of recovering your liberty, and of regaining your rightful place in the social scale, and if you neglect it, the blame will rest with yourselves. Strike the blow now, and you will all be free, all equally rich, all equally noble, and all be possessed of equal authority!"

At this juncture the whole scene presented a very singular and striking picture.

Stationed on the top of the mound which rose from the flat plain was the friar, seated on his mule, with his cowl thrown back on his shoulders, and his features inflamed by excitement.

Immediately beneath him were the two insurgent leaders, with Conrad Basset, Hothbrand, and several others, all on horseback.

Not far from them stood Frideswide, accoutred in breast-plate and casque, and bearing a two-handed sword on her broad shoulders.

Near the Amazon, and completely dwarfed by her, were Liripipe, Grouthead, Curthose, and the rest of the Dartford men.

Round and about stood the vast, disorderly host, with their wild, fierce visages turned towards the friar.

Those nearest him listened to his discourse, but those at a distance shouted loudly.

The background of the picture was formed by the walls of the ancient city and the lofty spire of the majestic cathedral.

When the friar descended from the mound, Wat Tyler rode up to his place, and drawing his sword, cried out, in a voice that was heard by all, "To Rochester Castle!"

A tremendous shout answered him, and immediately afterwards the whole host set off.

During their march to Rochester, which occupied the whole of the day, they conducted themselves as if they were in an enemy's country, plundering several large mansions, and two or three convents, and slaying all who resisted them.

Nor did their leaders attempt to check ferocity and licence.

Of course the hamlets, consisting only of

cottages of the peasantry, were respected, but all larger habitations were pillaged.

Thus, like a swarm of locusts, did the insurgents sweep on, devouring all before them, and spreading terror and confusion throughout the country.

They did not enter Faversham, but passed through Chartham and Chilham, and along the foot of the hills, and somewhat late in the evening reached Rochester, where they were warmly welcomed by the inhabitants.

Sir John de Newtoun, constable of the castle, was at once summoned to surrender, but as he hanged the messenger sent to him, preparations were made for the assault on the morrow.

END OF BOOK THE FIRST.

BOOK II.

THE YOUNG KING.

I.

EDITHA IS APPOINTED ONE OF THE PRINCESS'S ATTENDANTS.

AFTER her encounter with the insurgents outside the walls of Canterbury, the Princess of Wales continued her journey with the utmost expedition, and made no halt till she reached Dartford.

On arriving there, she alighted at St. Edmond's chantry, and, entering the little fane without any of her attendants, knelt down at the altar, and offered up heartfelt thanks for her deliverance from the rebels, concluding with an earnest prayer that their evil design might be defeated.

As she subsequently rode through the

village, on her way to the priory, where she intended to pass an hour with Lady Isabel, the few inhabitants left behind treated her with the utmost respect. Her ladies only accompanied her to the nunnery; all her male attendants, including Chaucer and Messer Benedetto, were sent to the hostel.

The Prioress was greatly rejoiced to see her, and heartily congratulated her on her escape. After partaking of some refreshment, the Princess had a private interview with the Lady Isabel in the locutory. Her first inquiries were concerning Editha, and she was not surprised to hear that the young damsel had sought an asylum in the priory.

"When I offered, on a former occasion, to take her into my household," she said, "you seemed opposed to the plan. Are you still of the same opinion?"

"No," replied the Prioress. "Were your

Highness to renew your gracious proposal, I would gladly accept it."

"I think you judge wisely," said the Princess. "With me she will be out of this daring rebel's power, should he attempt to regain possession of her. Since you agree to my proposal, I will take her with me now."

"It will be hard to part with her," sighed the Prioress; "but I will not allow my feelings to influence me. She shall go with you."

So saying, she struck the bell, and the summons was instantly answered by Sister Eudoxia.

"Did Editha come hither?" she said.

When the young damsel appeared, and had made an obeisance to the Princess, who received her as graciously as before, she told her what had been arranged.

"Must I then leave you, holy mother?"

cried Editha, unable to repress her tears. "Think me not ungrateful, gracious madam, if I seem loth to go," she added, to the Princess, "but I have been so happy here. I have never desired to stray beyond these walls; and now, less than ever."

"'Tis best you should go, child," said the Lady Isabel, controlling her emotion. "In the troublous times that are likely to occur, you will be safer with the Princess than with me. I gladly, therefore, commit you to her care."

"But may I not return to you again?" cried Editha.

"Certainly," said the Princess. "I shall not detain you against your inclinations."

"When you are accustomed to Court life, child," said the Prioress, gravely, yet kindly, "you will not desire to return to me."

To prevent further remonstrance, she added, quickly—

"But time presses. You must prepare for your journey."

"An instant!" cried Editha. Then, addressing the Princess, she said, "Perchance your Highness may not have heard what has happened since your departure?"

"Yes, I have told her all," remarked the Lady Isabel.

"Fear nothing," said the Princess. "Henceforth you will be under my protection."

Editha, however, still clung to the Prioress, and would gladly have remained with her; but finding this impossible, she bade her farewell.

"Farewell, my beloved child!" cried the Lady Isabel, embracing her affectionately. "I shall not forget you in my prayers. May all good saints watch over you!"

With a heart too full for utterance, Editha then left the room.

"Rest easy, Isabel," said the Princess, who was much touched by the scene. "I will be a mother to her."

It was an additional distress to Editha that she could not take leave of her mother, for it chanced that Dame Tyler was not at the priory on that day, and there was not time enough to send for her. However, Sister Eudoxia undertook to convey to her her daughter's tenderest adieux.

Editha did not see the Prioress again before her departure. Calm as she seemed, the Lady Isabel would not trust herself to another interview; but sent a message to the young damsel by Sister Eudoxia. It was simply this:—

"Come back when you will. Your cell shall always be kept for you."

As to Sister Eudoxia, she managed to put some constraint upon herself till Editha was gone; but when she had seen the last of her she burst into a flood of tears. All the sisters, indeed, were grieved to lose the young damsel, who was a general favourite; and many a wistful eye followed her as she rode off with the Princess's train.

Since other arrangements could not be made, she was placed on a pillion behind one of the grooms.

II.

ELTHAM PALACE.

SO sad was the young damsel, that for more than an hour she scarcely noticed any object; but at length she became aware that they were mounting a beautifully wooded hill, and on reaching its summit, a magnificent prospect burst upon her.

From the lofty eminence gained by the cavalcade she looked down upon a dark, heathy plain, stretching far and wide, and, even then, known as Blackheath.

On the right, this plain was bounded by the royal park and domain of Greenwich. But her eye rested not long on heath or park, but followed the course of the Thames, now illuminated by the setting sun, to London, which she beheld for the first time.

Struck with wonder at the sight, she could scarcely believe it real. Yes; there was the great city of which she had heard so much. There was the grim old Tower, with its strong walls and battlements, and its frowning keep, with the royal standard floating above it. There was the ancient bridge, with its many narrow, pointed arches, its fortified gates at either end, and picturesque old habitations closely packed between the gates. There was old St. Paul's, with its massive roof and its lofty spire shooting to the sky. Beyond was the Savoy, the palatial residence of John of Gaunt, the proud Duke of Lancaster. Other noble mansions, monastic buildings and churches, there were on either side of the river, but nothing that charmed the young damsel so much as the distant Abbey of Westminster.

Seeing how interested she was with the view, Chaucer, who was riding a little in advance, drew in the rein, and pointed out to her all the principal structures. But she needed not the poet's information, for she had recognised them at once.

While they were conversing, a large castellated mansion, hitherto screened by trees, suddenly came in sight; and as she glanced at Chaucer to inquire its designation, he told her it was the Palace of Eltham.

"The palace was built more than a hundred years ago," he said, "and ever since its completion it has been a royal residence. Henry the Third kept his Christmas here in 1269; and some fifteen years ago our late redoubted sovereign, Edward the Third, entertained here the captive, John of France. A magnificent entertainment it was, and worthy of the great monarch. We had a tournament, at which the King himself, with the Prince of Wales and all the royal dukes, jousted; and a ball, at which all the fairest dames of the Court were present. Never before, or since, have I beheld so many lovely women as on that occasion. There was one surpassingly beautiful person present, who is now buried in a convent."

Editha did not notice the latter observation, but said, "Does the Princess make Eltham Palace her chief residence?"

"Generally, she is with the Court, wherever it may be—at Windsor, Shene, Westminster, or the Tower—but she is often here. One reason why she is so much attached to the place is, that she spent many happy hours here with her valiant consort, the Black Prince."

"I do not wonder at it," said Editha. "Ah, I should have liked to see that brave Prince."

"You may see one who is equally brave,

though he has not earned such distinction—his brother, the Duke of Lancaster. Besides, you will see his son, the King."

"Does the King resemble his noble sire?" asked Edith.

"Not much," replied Chaucer. "He is more like the Princess, his mother."

"Then he must be very handsome."

"I doubt not you will think so, fair damsel," observed Chaucer, with a smile.

By this time they were close upon the palace, and a trumpet was blown to announce the Princess's approach.

It was a vast and stately edifice, comprehending four quadrangles, entirely surrounded by high walls, and an unusually broad and deep moat. Access was given to the palace, at the north and south, by a stone bridge with three arches, each bridge being protected by an embattled and turreted gateway.

Besides a noble banqueting-hall, the palace contained a chapel and a magnificent suite of state apartments.

A fair pleasance and a large tilt-yard were attached to the mansion, and the royal demesnes comprehended no less than three parks, each well timbered and well stocked with deer.

Passing through the gate, which was thrown wide open by the halberdiers stationed at it, and crossing the bridge, the Princess rode into the principal court, where a crowd of servants, in the royal liveries, with a chamberlain at their head, having a gold chain round his neck, and bearing a white wand, were waiting to receive her.

Already tidings had been received at the palace of the rising at Dartford, and the march of the rebels to Rochester; and much anxiety being felt for the royal lady, her safe arrival was hailed with the greatest satisfaction.

These sentiments were conveyed to her by the chamberlain in a lengthened address, which, perhaps, the occasion might warrant, but which proved somewhat tedious.

Before dismounting, the Princess despatched a mounted messenger to the King, her son, who was then at the Tower, to inform him of her safe return to Eltham, and begging him to come to her early on the morrow, as she had matter of the utmost import to communicate to him.

After expressing their deep obligations to the Princess, Chaucer and Benedetto would now have taken leave of her Highness; but she desired them to stay, that they might recount their adventures with the rebels to the King.

"Having been eye-witnesses of the proceedings of these lawless men, you are the fittest persons to give his Majesty a description of them," she said. "Remain with me till to-morrow, I pray you."

These arrangements made, the Princess alighted, and entered the palace with her ladies.

The delay that had occurred afforded Editha an opportunity of looking round the quadrangle, and she was greatly struck by its magnitude and beauty; while she could easily perceive, through open archways, that there were other courts beyond, proving the great extent of the palace.

That it was splendidly kept up was shown by the number of retainers. But the young damsel was positively enraptured when she beheld the grand banqueting-hall, with its richly carved screen, its gallery for minstrels, its magnificent open timber roof, and unequalled bay windows.

So overpowered was she when she followed the Princess and her ladies into this matchless hall that she could scarcely draw breath. Some idea of its size, though not of its beauty, may be formed, when we mention that it was upwards of a hundred feet long, proportionately wide, and nearly fifty feet in height; the enormous rafters being of chestnut.

After partaking of some refreshments, the Princess passed into the state apartments, and thence to her private rooms. She had treated Editha with marked kindness and consideration, and she now assigned her a small chamber communicating with her own rooms, and gave orders that she should be provided with suitable attire.

Fatigued with her journey, and exhausted by the anxiety she had undergone, the Princess retired early to rest, but not before she had attended complines in the chapel.

When Editha appeared next morning,

arrayed in the attire provided for her, every one was astonished by her beauty.

She no longer looked like a simple country maiden. Her slender figure was charmingly displayed by a tight-fitting côte hardie of green velvet; a gold girdle, from which hung a long chain of the same metal, loosely encircled her waist; and round her fair tresses was bound a snowy covrechef, that imparted additional softness to her features.

Ever accustomed to early devotional exercises at the Priory, she attended matins in the chapel, and then, finding that the Princess was with her confessor in the oratory, she went forth into the pleasance.

III.

RICHARD OF BORDEAUX.

TEMPTED to extend her walk by the extreme beauty of the morning, she crossed the north bridge, passed the barbacan, and entered the park.

She had not proceeded far, when the splendid panorama she had previously contemplated opened before her.

Once more her eyes ranged over Blackheath, traced the course of the river, and settled upon the distant city.

Once more she was gazing upon the Tower, and the ancient bridge adjoining it, when her attention was suddenly called to a small party of horsemen, who had just entered the avenue and were coming quickly along it.

At the head of the party rode a noble-looking youth, so splendidly arrayed, and mounted on a charger so richly trapped, that Editha could not doubt it was the young King.

Uncertain whether to proceed or return, she stood still; and, during that interval, the princely horseman, who was coming swiftly on, drew near.

She could now clearly discern that his blue velvet mantle, lined with ermine, was embroidered all over, and fastened at the neck with a diamond clasp; that his tunic was of cloth of silver; his girdle studded with jewels, as was the hilt of his poniard; and his velvet cap richly ornamented with precious stones.

The trappings of his charger were of blue velvet, decorated with the royal badge of the white hart, with the letter R worked in silver, proving, beyond doubt, that it was the King.

So finely cut and delicate were the youthful monarch's features, so smooth and blooming his cheeks, so long the brown locks that fell down upon his shoulders, so slight his figure, that he almost looked a damsel in male attire, especially when contrasted with the three nobles who followed him, all of whom were strongly made, and had manly visages.

These knightly personages were the Baron de Vertain, Sir Simon Burley, and Sir Eustace de Valletort. The latter has already been described as the lord to whom Wat Tyler was vassal, and from whom he received his freedom.

Sir Eustace had been a great favourite with the Black Prince, and was one of those to whom the hero, when dying, committed the care of his son. Sir Eustace had discharged the trust as faithfully as he could.

Though the valiant knight had seen hard

service in France, Brittany, and Castile, and had now reached the middle term of life, he was still full of vigour, and exceedingly handsome. His attire was not so extravagant as that of De Vertain, who glittered in diamonds and rich stuffs, and wore particoloured hose and cracowes, like a Court popinjay as he was, but he could not compare with De Valletort.

Sir Simon Burley was somewhat older than De Valletort, but a noble-looking personage.

Behind rode three esquires, and as many pages, all extremely well mounted, and apparelled in the royal livery.

The young King was not yet sixteen. Born on the Feast of the Epiphany, in 1367, he was surnamed, from the place of his birth, Richard of Bordeaux. He was baptized by the Archbishop of Bordeaux, in the Church of St. Andrew, in that fair city; the

Bishop of Agen and the King of Minorca being his godfathers.

Singularly beautiful as a child, and full of quickness and intelligence, Richard gave early promise of high and noble qualities; but he had the misfortune to lose his illustrious father, the Lord Edward of England, before his character was fully formed; and, indeed, the long and painful illness, sometimes attributed to poison, from which the Black Prince suffered, prevented him from bestowing sufficient care on his son. But he felt the deepest anxiety on his account, knowing the dangers he would be exposed to from the designs of his ambitious uncles, and his last thoughts were of Richard.

On the day after the death of his grandsire, Edward III., Richard, then in his eleventh year, rode, in solemn state, from the Palace of Westminster to the City of London. The superb procession was preceded by trumpeters, who made the streets ring with the bruit of their clarions.

Before the youthful King rode his uncle, the Duke of Lancaster and the Duke of Northumberland. The sword of state was borne by Sir Simon Burley; and the royal charger, trapped in cloth of gold, and having a splendid plume of feathers on its head, was led by Sir Nicholas Bond. Richly arrayed pages walked on either side.

Clad in white velvet, the youthful monarch charmed all the beholders by his grace and beauty of feature. His retinue was composed of a vast number of nobles, knights, and esquires, all richly apparelled.

On his entrance into the City, Richard was met by the Lord Mayor, the Sheriffs, and the Aldermen, in their robes, accompanied by a great body of citizens on horseback, and making a very goodly show.

After being warmly welcomed by the

civic authorities, the young King rode slowly through the streets, amid the ceaseless acclamations of the assembled multitude. The conduits flowed with wine; temples and triumphal arches were everywhere reared; the houses were hung with tapestry and cloth of arras; and nothing was heard but joyous shouts, mingled with strains of music and the loud braying of trumpets.

The grandest pageant was at Cheapside, where a mimic castle of great size was erected, on the four turrets of which stood beautiful damsels, all of the same age as the young King, and arrayed in vestments of white.

On the arrival of the royal procession, these lovely young damsels showered leaves of gold upon the young King and those with him; and then, descending from their elevated position, served them with wine in cups of gold.

But this was not all. By means of some ingenious mechanism, which we pretend not to describe, an angel flew down from the summit of the castle, and placed a circle of gold on the young King's brow.

Everywhere received with demonstrations of loyalty and affection, Richard quitted the City, highly gratified by his visit.

As soon as the late King's obsequies were finished, Richard was crowned with extraordinary splendour at Westminster Abbey, the ceremony being performed by Simon de Sudbury, Archbishop of Canterbury, in the presence of the King's three uncles, the Duke of Lancaster, the Earls of Cambridge and Buckingham, the barons, all the great officers of the Crown, abbots, and prelates.

No previous coronation had been so splendid, and it was hoped that it portended a prosperous and brilliant reign.

But the King, being a minor, many years

must needs elapse before he himself could assume the reins of government; and these years were fraught with peril.

A Council of Regency was appointed, of which his uncles were members, the Duke of Lancaster being the real head.

Serious events soon occurred. Hostilities were renewed with France and Spain, and the truce with Scotland was broken. The new wars occasioned enormous expenditure. Large subsidies had to be raised, and the burdens of the people were increased by the intolerable imposts. To make matters worse, the wars were not successful.

For the first few years of the young King's reign, ample grants were obtained; but the demands were so incessant that loud complaints were made, and petitions sent to Parliament, praying for the dismissal of the Ministers.

Despite all efforts to remove them, they

remained in power, and continued their exactions. Fresh taxes were levied, rendered especially obnoxious by the mode of their collection; and these led to the rising we have described.

Richard's education was purposely neglected by his uncles. Sir Simon Burley, who was beloved by his father and trusted by his grandfather, had been appointed his tutor. But he had not sufficient authority to control his royal pupil. His counsels were disregarded, his reproofs derided.

However, the young King was well versed in all manly exercises—in tilting, archery, wrestling, and delighted in field sports, in which he was allowed freely to indulge. Moreover, he was a perfect horseman.

Though endowed with excellent qualities, and possessing a generous disposition, Richard was wayward and self-willed, and, even at that early age, addicted to pleasureable pursuits. Inclined to be a great coxcomb, he was extravagantly fond of dress, and loaded himself with jewellery. For one robe of cloth of gold, adorned with precious stones, he gave thirty thousand marks.

He was surrounded by flatterers somewhat older than himself, who encouraged his frivolous and extravagant tastes, and counterbalanced the wholesome advice of his mother.

Still, though grievously disappointed, the Princess did not despair, but persuaded herself that her son's nobler qualities would be developed as he grew older, and that he would eventually become worthy of the great name he bore.

Sir Simon Burley and Sir Eustace de Valletort were with the young King at the Tower when he received his mother's message, praying him to come to her at

Eltham on the morrow, and they urged him to obey the summons.

Though the thoughtless young monarch was not so much alarmed as his attendants by the reports he had heard of the insurrection, he was curious to hear some account of it from his mother's lips.

He therefore resolved to go to her, and ordered Sir Simon and Sir Eustace to attend him. He also decided upon taking with him the Baron de Vertain, who was an especial favourite.

The royal party set out from the Tower betimes, and reached Eltham much earlier than was expected.

IV.

THE MEETING BETWEEN THE YOUNG KING AND EDITHA.

AFTER a momentary indecision, as we have described, Editha thought it best to turn back, but was presently overtaken by the young King, who graciously returned the obeisance she made him; and, being much struck by her appearance, drew in the rein, and addressed her.

"Give you good morrow, fair damsel!" he cried, in a blithe voice. "I marvel not you have come forth early, seeing the morning is so enchanting. I have much enjoyed my ride across the heath. I had no idea it was so pleasant."

"It looks delightful, my liege," observed Editha, timidly.

"You are one of the Princess's attendants, I suppose, and have just returned with her from Canterbury?" remarked the King.

"Only from Dartford, my liege," she replied.

"From Dartford!" exclaimed Richard. "That was where the insurrection commenced. You must have witnessed it. Were you not greatly frightened?"

"I saw very little of it, my liege. I took refuge in the priory, and the rebels quitted the village immediately, and marched on to Rochester."

"'Tis well our mother did not encounter them!" cried the King.

"Indeed, my liege, her Grace did encounter them yesterday, near Canterbury," replied Editha.

"Ha! Did they offer her any rudeness?" exclaimed Richard, quickly.

"No; they treated her with great respect," she replied.

"Then they are not such graceless villains as we deemed them!" cried the King, laughing. "You hear what this damsel says, my lords?" he added, turning to his attendants who were close behind him.

"We do, my liege, and are rejoiced to learn that her Grace sustained no injury," observed the Baron de Vertain. "Had it been otherwise, we would have hanged them all."

"Then you must have hanged some thousands," observed Sir Simon Burley. "'Tis most fortunate her Grace escaped so well."

"Neither she nor her ladies were in any way molested," remarked Editha.

While this colloquy took place, Sir Eustace de Valletort had been earnestly regarding Editha, and he now addressed her.

"The leader of the Dartford rebels is a smith, named Wat Tyler, is he not?" he inquired, looking at her fixedly.

"There are several leaders," she replied. "More than half the village joined the insurgents."

"I will not ask you how the insurrection originated," said Sir Simon. "We know that a tax-collector was slain."

"He deserved his fate, if all we have heard be true," interposed Sir Eustace. "The damsel has already told us that she sought refuge in the priory."

"'Twas the safest place to choose," said the King.

V.

SIR EUSTACE DE VALLETORT OBTAINS SOME INFORMATION FROM THE PRINCESS.

NOT expecting the King at such an early hour, the Princess was at mass at the time of his arrival; but as soon as her devotions were finished she repaired with her ladies to the great hall, where she found him at breakfast with his attendants.

Richard immediately arose from the table, and flying to meet her, bent the knee and kissed her hand. This act of filial respect performed, his mother tenderly embraced him.

After she had received the congratulations of Sir Simon Burley and the others on her escape from the rebels, she was ceremoniously conducted by her son to the table, which was on a daïs at the upper end of the hall.

The Princess sat on the King's right, and, next to her, on the other side, was Sir Eustace de Valletort. All her ladies occupied seats at the upper table.

On the King's left were De Vertain and Sir Simon Burley. Chaucer and Benedetto were placed at the lower table. As yet they had no opportunity of conferring with the King. By her Grace's express orders, Editha was stationed behind the Princess's chair.

The Princess's account of her meeting with the insurgents was listened to with the greatest interest, and with evident uneasiness, by Sir Simon Burley and De Valletort; but Richard, who seemed surprised and rather amused that Sir John Holland and the young nobles should return to Canterbury, did not attach much importance to the insurrection, and expressed an opinion that it would very soon be quelled.

"What can these wretched peasants do?" he cried. "Sir John and his little band ought to have scattered them like sheep!"

"Sir John thought differently," remarked the Princess, gravely. "The insurgents are stubborn and resolute, and better armed than your Majesty seems to suppose. It will be prudent and proper to make terms with them."

"Make terms with rebels! That we shall never do!" exclaimed Richard, scornfully.

"I mean that the grievances of which they justly complain must be redressed," said his mother.

"I did not know that they had any grievances," cried Richard, with a careless laugh. "I fancied they were rather too well treated by their lords."

"So they are, my liege," observed De

Vertain. "They are far better treated than they deserve."

"Not so, my lord," said the Princess. "They do not complain without reason. They are much oppressed, and the King will be badly advised if he does not listen to their prayers."

"They must address their prayers to the Council, not to me, madam," said Richard. "I do not tax them."

"But they say your Majesty will ruin the kingdom by your extravagance," remarked De Vertain.

"Ha! say they so? Then—by my father's head!—I will grant none of their petitions! Am I to be checked in my expenditure by these sordid scoundrels?"

"Certainly not, my liege," observed De Vertain. "That were a rare jest"

"Yet it may happen in right earnest," said Sir Simon Burley.

"It *will* happen, if you continue to turn a deaf ear to the complaints of your subjects!" said the Princess. "This young damsel," she added, signing to Editha to come forward, "whom I have brought with me from Dartford, will tell you how much discontent prevails among the peasantry."

"She can have had no opportunity for observation," remarked the King.

"Pardon me, my liege; I have had every opportunity," said Editha. "I have seen and heard much; and I venture to affirm, in your royal presence, that the people have just cause for complaint. This wicked and treasonable rising would never have occurred had their prayers been listened to."

"Our mother has taught you this lesson!" laughed Richard, incredulously.

"No; 'tis from her I have learnt it," said the Princess.

"You surprise me!" said the King. "I

should not have supposed she would trouble herself with such matters. Pray, who is this fair damsel who has contrived to obtain so much important information?"

"She is the daughter of the chief leader of the insurrection," replied the Princess.

Every one now looked astonished, and the King most of all.

"Wat Tyler's daughter!" he exclaimed. "By St. Edward, I cannot believe it!"

"It must be a jest, my liege!" muttered De Vertain.

"I am not in a mood for jesting," said the Princess, who had overheard the remark. "As I have stated, Editha is the rebel leader's daughter. But let me add, that when the outbreak occurred, she sought an asylum with the Prioress of St. Mary, by whom she was yesterday committed to my care."

"I trust she does not share her father's

sentiments," observed Richard. "Nay; I am certain she is no rebel," he added quickly, perceiving that the young damsel looked much pained by the observation.

"Your Majesty has not a more loyal subject than myself," cried Editha, earnestly.

"Enough!" said Richard. "Had you been otherwise than loyal, I should have distrusted my own skill in physiognomy. Never, I am sure, could a treasonable thought be harboured in that gentle breast!"

"You only do her justice, my son," observed the Princess

"May I ask your Grace a question?" said Sir Eustace de Valletort, in a low voice, to the Princess. "You say this fair damsel is Wat Tyler's daughter?"

"She passes for his daughter," replied the Princess, in an under tone, and with a certain significance. "But no one can look at her and doubt that she is of gentle birth. She has been brought up in a cottage, and as the offspring of those who have had the care of her."

"But you mentioned the Prioress of St. Mary," remarked Sir Eustace, with tremulous eagerness. "Does she take an interest in Editha—as I think this damsel is named?"

"She has been as a mother to her!" replied the Princess.

Sir Eustace said no more, and avoided the look fixed upon him.

Shortly afterwards, silver ewers filled with rose-water, and napkins, were brought by the attendants. On rising from the table, the Princess was conducted by her royal son to the state apartments.

VI.

SIR SIMON BURLEY.

PASSING through a gallery, occupying one side of the great quadrangle, and in which stood a vast number of richly-clad retainers, the Princess and her royal son, followed by all the company, entered a stately apartment, more than a hundred feet in length, and adorned with tapestry from the finest Flemish looms, representing boar hunts, wolf hunts, and scenes of hawking.

At the upper end of this magnificent apartment was an estrade, surmounted by a crimson velvet canopy, embroidered in gold with roses, and the royal cognizance of the White Hart.

On the estrade were two royal seats, designed for the King and his mother, when a council should be held, or some important personage be received by them in state.

But the Princess did not now proceed beyond the centre of the chamber, where the company assembled.

Desirous of having a private conference with her son, she took him and Sir Simon Burley into the recess of a deep bay-window; and as soon as they were out of hearing, begged the old knight to state his opinion frankly as to the insurrection.

"Madam," replied Sir Simon, gravely, "I have already given my opinion to the King. I believe it to be the most dangerous outbreak that has ever menaced the State! Nor do I see how it can be quelled. For the present it is confined to two counties— Kent and Essex; but I fear it will spread throughout the whole kingdom. A circumstance has just happened to me, which I will relate to you, as it shows the extreme audacity of the insurgents. A burgher of Gravesend, named Thurstan, who is a bondman of mine, solicited his freedom from me. I demanded four hundred marks; and as he refused to pay the money, I sent him a prisoner to Rochester Castle. When taken there, he told the Constable, Sir John de Newtoun, that he would soon be set free. And it is certain he must have found some means of communicating with the rebels; for when they came to Rochester, they sent a message to the Constable, demanding Thurstan's immediate release; adding, that if he were not given up to them, they would storm the castle and take him."

"And I much fear they will try to execute the threat," remarked the Princess.

"Sir John de Newtoun will laugh at them," said the King. "I hope he will hang Thurstan from the walls of the castle, and bid the rebels take him down, if they want him."

"That would only enrage them the more, and cause them to proceed to dire extremities," said the Princess.

"You are right, madam," rejoined Sir Simon.

"Rochester is one of our strongest castles, and can hold out against a legion of badly armed peasants," cried the King.

"But it may be taken by treachery, and that is what is to be apprehended," said Burley.

"Methinks you greatly overrate the danger, Sir Simon," said Richard. "What can the people do against the nobles and knights?"

"That question will have to be answered at the point of the sword, sire," replied Burley. "Unluckily, we have no army to oppose them."

"What!" cried Richard, in astonishment. "Is an army required to quell an outbreak of peasants?"

"Sire," replied Sir Simon, "we know not whom to trust. As yet, we cannot tell who are loyal, and who traitors. This conspiracy—for a conspiracy it is—has been so well contrived, and kept so secret, that it cannot have been the work of a common hand. Some important personage must have been concerned in it. I scarcely dare breathe my suspicions, but I think——"

And he hesitated.

"Speak out!" cried the King. "You suspect one of our uncles? It cannot be the Duke of Lancaster. He is at Roxburgh."

"I suspect the Earl of Buckingham, my liege," replied Sir Simon. "He is thought to be in Wales; but some one much resembling him has been seen in Essex since this rebellion broke out."

"You never hinted this to me before," said the King.

"I only received the information late last night, my liege, and meant not to repeat it till it should be confirmed. But I think it best not to keep it back, that your Majesty may be aware of the magnitude of the danger."

"If our uncle of Buckingham is conspiring against us, the danger is, indeed, great," said the King. "But I cannot think it."

"I have already warned you against him," said the Princess.

For a moment a shade came over Richard's countenance, but it quickly disappeared.

His mother and Sir Simon watched him anxiously.

"A council ought to be held without delay," observed the Princess. "Would it could be held here!"

"I have anticipated your wishes, madam,"

replied Burley. "Before quitting the Tower this morning, I despatched messengers to the Archbishop of Canterbury at Lambeth Palace, and to the Lord Treasurer at his manor of Highbury, acquainting them both with the perilous state of things, and telling them they would find his Majesty at Eltham, with your Grace."

"You did well, Sir Simon," said the Princess, approvingly. "The Chancellor of the realm and the Lord Treasurer are best able to advise at such critical conjuncture."

"I have taken another step, of which I hope his Majesty will approve," pursued Burley. "Having heard that some of the citizens are disaffected, I have summoned Sir William Walworth, the Lord Mayor, and Sir John Philpot, to attend, in order that his Majesty may learn the exact truth. Both are thoroughly loyal and trustworthy, and can be relied on in this emergency."

"I know it," replied Richard; "I have perfect faith in them. But I will not distrust the good citizens of London. Whenever I have gone among them they have received me with demonstrations of loyalty and regard. You cannot fail to remember my first visit to the City, Sir Simon, and the welcome given me on that occasion?"

"I remember it well, my liege," replied Burley. "But things have changed since then. However, we shall hear what the Mayor has to say."

Just then an usher, bearing a white wand, made his appearance, and, bowing profoundly, informed the King that the Lord Mayor and Sir John Philpot had just arrived at the palace.

"They are heartily welcome," cried Richard. "Bring them to our presence forthwith, and take care that their attendants are well entertained."

"They have obeyed the summons quickly," observed the Princess.

Scarcely was the usher gone, when the chamberlain appeared, and announced the arrival of the Archbishop of Canterbury and the Lord High Treasurer, Sir Robert Hales.

"Our council will be complete," said the King, repeating the order he had just given to the usher. "Come, madam, let us take our seats," he added to the Princess.

"Before holding the council," she rejoined, "had you not better confer with Master Geoffrey Chaucer and Messer Benedetto? Both have been captives of the rebels, and have much to relate, which it is needful your Majesty should hear."

"Let them relate it to the council," said Richard. "Bid them follow us," he added, to Sir Simon.

Leading the Princess to the estrade, he

placed her on one of the royal chairs, and seated himself beside her.

The Baron de Vertain and Sir Eustace de Valletort stationed themselves on the right of the King, while Sir Simon Burley, with Chaucer and Benedetto, stood on the left.

The general company did not move from the centre of the apartment, and between them and the royal seats were grouped a number of richly clad attendants.

VII.

SIR WILLIAM WALWORTH AND SIR JOHN PHILPOT.

PRESENTLY a stir was heard at the lower end of the room, and two striking-looking personages, preceded by an usher, could be seen making their way through the assemblage.

The foremost was the Lord Mayor.

Above the ordinary height, strongly built, but extremely well-proportioned, Sir William Walworth had features of the true Saxon type. His locks were of light brown; his beard of the same colour. His eyes were of a clear grey, quick and penetrating.

The habitual expression of his countenance was frank, good-humoured, and cordial; but he could look stern enough when severity was needed. His frame showed that he possessed great personal strength, and he was a proficient in all martial exercises. Though a merchant, Sir William was half a soldier, and had a considerable body of armed men under him. Indeed, a strong escort had attended him to the palace.

The Lord Mayor wore a dark blue velvet gown, bordered with fur, and his côtehardie was of the same stuff. Round his neck was the collar of SS, and from his girdle hung a dagger, destined to become historical.

Sir William Walworth was a wealthy London merchant, and much esteemed by his fellow-citizens for his high character. He was a member of the Fishmongers' Company, and when he was advanced to the mayoralty, a pageant of extraordinary splendour was exhibited by them in his honour. At a subsequent date his statue was placed in the great hall of the Company, within a niche behind the chair of the Prime Warden.

Sir John Philpot was another renowned and wealthy London merchant. About three years prior to the date of our story, he performed a singularly daring action, to which some allusion has already been made.

When the war broke out again in Scotland, a bold pirate, named Mercer, who had several armed vessels under his command, carried off a fleet of merchantmen from Scarborough. No effort being made by the Council to capture this pirate, who continued to scour the North Sea with impunity, Sir John Philpot armed a small squadron at his own cost, and went in quest of him.

Captain Mercer was easily found, and quite ready to give battle to the brave citizen, who at once attacked him, and capturing him and all his vessels, brought them into the port of London.

For this gallant and patriotic act he was reprimanded by the Council, who forbade him to wage war on his own account; but he little recked the reproof, feeling he had earned the gratitude of his fellow-citizens.

Quite as tall as Sir William Walworth, and quite as powerfully made, the brave knight, though plain of feature, had an open, manly countenance, characterized by great firmness of expression.

His locks were grizzled, and his cheeks bronzed by exposure to the weather. His costume was devoid of ornament. He wore a furred gown, beneath which could be seen a velvet tunic. From his girdle hung a purse and a badélaire, or short broadsword.

As the Lord Mayor and his companion were ushered into the royal presence, and each had made a profound obeisance, Richard rose from his seat, and, descending a single step of the estrade, but no more, received them with great dignity of manner.

"Welcome, my good Lord Mayor!" he cried. "Welcome, also, my brave and falthful Sir John Philpot! Right glad are we to see you both at a moment when our throne is threatened by rebels! You bring us, we trust, good tidings, and can give us the assurance that all your fellow-citizens continue as loyal and well affected as they have ever heretofore shown themselves towards us. Is it so?"

Having said thus much, he resumed his seat.

"Sire," replied the Lord Mayor, in a firm voice, "I cannot answer the question you have deigned to put to me as satisfactorily as I could desire; but I will not attempt to disguise the truth, however unpalatable it may be to your Majesty. The bulk of the citizens of London are as loyal and devoted as ever; but I grieve to say there are many disaffected persons among them, who seek to incite the others to rise in opposition to your authority."

Richard uttered an exclamation of anger.

"How say you, Sir John Philpot?" he cried. "Do you confirm the Lord Mayor's statement? Do you believe the citizens of London—some few of them, I mean—are factious and seditious?"

"My liege, 'tis even so," replied Philpot. "Some evil influence hath been at work among them of late, and many loyal burghers have been turned from their duty."

"By whose agency have they been thus perverted, Sir John?" demanded the King, sharply.

" 'Twere dangerous to speak too plainly, my liege," he replied. "My suspicions must be for your Majesty's private ear."

" You hint not at a member of the Council, eh?"

" I hint at no one, my liege."

" Then speak plainly."

" Sir John has spoken as plainly as he can," remarked the Princess, in a low tone, to the King. "He dares not name your uncle, the Earl of Buckingham. You must question him in private."

" Thus much I will boldly declare to your Majesty," said Philpot; "and I will take the consequences on my own head. Some of those who have fomented this rebellion are not far to seek."

And as he spoke, he directed a glance at Chaucer, who was stationed near the King, as previously mentioned.

" If that false and calumnious charge is

made against me, Sir John, I can easily relieve myself from it," said the poet. "Messer Benedetto and myself have both been made prisoners by the rebels, and owe our deliverance from them solely to her Highness the Princess of Wales."

"You were at Dartford at the time of the outbreak," said Sir John, still looking fixedly at him. "You were seen in converse with the rebel leader."

"Nay, good Sir John, that proves nothing," interposed Benedetto. "I also was at Dartford at the time of the outbreak, and I likewise conversed with Wat Tyler. Moreover, I was made prisoner by another rebel leader, and should be in captivity now, and in peril of my life, had not the Princess graciously undertaken that I should pay a heavy ransom, which I shall do, of course, albeit the men are rebels."

"But you are not, like Master Geoffrey

Chaucer, a partisan of the Duke of Lancaster," observed Philpot.

"You have not forgiven the Duke, Sir John, because he reprimanded you for making war on your own account, in the case of the Scottish pirate, Mercer," observed Chaucer. "His Grace has no more to do with this insurrection than I have."

"Then he is greatly misrepresented, and so is the Earl of Buckingham, for the citizens make free with both their names," said Philpot. "Some are for John of Gaunt, some for Buckingham."

"But none for the King?" cried the Princess.

"Yes, madam," replied Philpot; "I spoke only of the disaffected. Beyond doubt, the majority of the citizens are still loyal."

An interruption was here offered by the chamberlain, who announced the Archbishop of Canterbury and the Lord Treasurer.

VIII.

THE ARCHBISHOP OF CANTERBURY AND THE LORD OF ST. JOHN'S.

IMON DE SUDBURY, Archbishop of Canterbury and Chancellor of England, was a very stately personage, his imposing appearance being heightened by the splendour of his vestments. His cope and dalmatic were covered with the richest embroidery and white silk; all being flowered with gold. His shoes and gloves were likewise richly embroidered, the latter being adorned at the back with jewels. A silk coif covered his head.

The Archbishop's person was lofty, his

expression proud, and his deportment extremely dignified.

A man of a very high order of intellect, and of admirable judgment on all matters, ecclesiastical or secular, Simon de Sudbury had exercised great influence in the state councils during the latter part of the previous reign, and was much regarded by Edward III.

Appointed Chancellor on the accession of Richard II., he had discharged the duties of his onerous office with the greatest ability and rectitude, though unfounded imputations were cast upon him by his enemies.

Since his elevation to the archiepiscopal throne, in 1374, Simon de Sudbury had conferred great benefits on Canterbury—had improved the internal condition of the cathedral, enlarged his palace, repaired the ruinous city walls, and built a new gate, which still remains to attest his worth.

Sir Robert Hales, Grand Master of St. John's Hospital, and Lord Treasurer, who accompanied the Archbishop, had a very austere countenance. Rarely, it would seem, did a smile light up his sharp features. An aquiline nose, eyes black and piercing, complexion sallow, cheeks scrupulously shaven, and dark locks closely shorn—such was his personal appearance.

Round his neck he wore a broad jewelled collar.

A long robe of black velvet, with loose sleeves, and bordered with sable, formed his costume. His cap was of black velvet, without ornament.

As the Archbishop and the Lord of St. John's approached, with slow and stately step, the Lord Mayor and Sir John Philpot drew on one side, while Richard descended from the estrade.

Bending reverently, the King did not rise

till the Archbishop had pronounced a benediction over him. He then thanked his Grace and the Lord Treasurer for so promptly attending to his summons.

"Never had we greater need of your wise and prudent counsel than now," he said.

"I have long dreaded this outbreak, my liege," rejoined the Archbishop; "but it has come upon us suddenly at the last. We ought to have been better prepared; we have had plenty of warnings."

"That is true, your Grace," said the King; "but the warnings have been disregarded. The question now before us is—how the rebellion can best be crushed. Come forward, I pray you, my Lord Mayor; and you, Sir John Philpot. We must have the advantage of your counsel. Sir Simon Burley, and Sir Eustace de Valletort, you must likewise lend us aid."

So saying, the King returned to his seat,

and the Archbishop stationed himself on his right hand. The others gathered round the foot of the estrade.

"Your Majesty has asked how this rebellion can best be crushed," said Sir Simon Burley. "'Tis a question, I fear, that none of us can answer satisfactorily. The moment for the outbreak has been so well chosen, that it finds us wholly unprepared. Our armies are in Brittany and Spain. To remove the forces from the North would expose us to an immediate invasion from Scotland. We have scarce men-at-arms enow for the defence of London. How, then, are we to attack the rebel host?"

"Two thousand men can be raised within the City of London," said Sir John Philpot; "and if his Majesty will give me the command of them, I will march at once against the rebels. If I disperse not the knaves, I will consent to lose my head!"

"Your proposition likes us well, Sir John," observed Richard. "How say you, my Lord Mayor, can you spare two thousand men?"

"No, my liege," replied Sir William Walworth. "Not half the number—not a third. As I have already intimated to your Majesty, there are many disaffected citizens, and these ill-disposed persons would assuredly rise in revolt were an opportunity afforded them, as it would be by the removal of the soldiery, who now keep them in restraint."

"You are right," observed Sir Simon Burley.

"Would that the Duke of Lancaster were here!" exclaimed Sir Robert Hales.

"He is better at Roxburgh," cried Philpot. "Were he here, he would be more likely to lead the rebels than to aid in routing them!"

"You malign his Grace!" cried the Lord Treasurer, indignantly. "Were he present you would not dare to make such a charge against him!"

"I will stand by my words!" said Philpot, boldly.

"The charge is false!" cried Chaucer, stepping forward; "as false as the accusation thou hast just brought against me of conspiring with the rebels at Dartford!"

"I have proof of what I have stated, that on the evening before the outbreak you had a private conference with the chief of the insurgents," rejoined Philpot. "I counsel his Majesty to keep you a close prisoner in the Tower till the rebellion be put down."

"I shall be content to remain a prisoner if his Majesty entertains any doubt of my loyalty."

"You are a known partisan of our uncle, good Master Chaucer," observed Richard.

"We shall be glad to have you with us at the Tower—not as a prisoner, but as a guest. You will, therefore, return with us."

Chaucer bowed, and retired. But he cast a menacing glance at Sir John Philpot.

"I would this poll-tax had never been imposed," observed the King. "It has led to most unfortunate results."

"'Tis not the tax that has caused the outbreak, my liege, though it may seem to have done so," rejoined the Archbishop. "The peasantry have long been discontented."

"And they have real grievances to complain of," remarked the Princess. "Since, as it now appears, his Majesty cannot find soldiery to put them down, will it not be best to treat with them, and grant their requests—provided they are not immoderate?"

"You say well, madam," rejoined the

Archbishop. " 'Twill be advisable to listen to their complaints. At all events, time will be gained."

" But they must not be deluded with false hopes, or they will become yet more embittered against us," said the Princess.

"Before his Majesty can make any promises to the insurgents, he must know what they ask—or, rather, demand," observed the Treasurer.

" True," replied the Princess. " But I would have him meet them in a conciliatory spirit."

" In his negotiations with the rebels, his Majesty must be entirely governed by their conduct towards him," said the Archbishop. "A favourable hearing may be granted to petitions and entreaties, but he cannot yield to threats."

" Never!" cried Richard. " I would die sooner!"

"I like not the notion of treating with rebels," observed Sir Simon Burley. "But it appears to me that we have no option."

"Nay; it is certain we must either fight them or treat with them!" cried Sir Eustace de Valletort. "For my own part, I would rather fight them!"

"Where are they now?" demanded the Lord Mayor.

"They were at Canterbury yesterday," replied Sir Simon. "And, doubtless, they are there still, unless the inhabitants have expelled them."

"The inhabitants, I fear, will take part with them," said the Archbishop. "Many of them are as disaffected as the citizens of London have been described to be by the Lord Mayor."

"I am sorry to hear your Grace say so," observed the Princess. "I fancied the city was as loyal as any in England. Should it be as your Grace represents, I fear my son, Sir John Holland, and the young nobles with him, may be in some danger."

"Did you leave them there, madam?" inquired the Archbishop.

"They were compelled to take refuge in the city, in order to avoid the insurgents," she replied.

"And you have had no tidings of them since?"

"None, your Grace."

"You need have no uneasiness on their account, madam," remarked the King. "Sir John Holland has just made his appearance. You may see him, with some of his attendants, at the lower end of the room. He will bring us the last news of the rebels."

"I am right glad to see him. I own I felt much uneasiness on his account," said the Princess.

Next moment Sir John Holland approached the royal circle.

It was evident, from the state of his attire, that he had ridden fast and far, and his appearance excited a strong feeling of anxiety among the persons around the King.

He was followed by Sir Osbert Montacute, looking equally exhausted.

IX.

THE BARON DE VERTAIN AND SIR JOHN PHILPOT PROPOSE TO ATTACK THE REBELS.

RICHARD immediately arose, and, embracing his half-brother, congratulated him heartily on his escape from the rebels.

"Our escape has been accomplished with the greatest difficulty, my liege," replied Sir John Holland. "We owe our preservation to the Abbot of St. Augustine, who got us safely out of the city, and provided us with horses. Canterbury is in the hands of the rebels, and had we been captured we should have been put to death without mercy."

As he thus spoke, the Princess could not repress her agitation, and those near the King looked at each other in dismay.

"Ha! by St. George! do the villains dare to proceed to these extremities?" exclaimed Richard.

"My liege, they are fiends let loose," said Sir John. "Already they have done incalculable mischief. Your Grace's palace has been besieged and plundered."

"I care not for my own losses," replied the Archbishop, "provided my household and retainers are uninjured."

"The wretches have displayed a most vindictive spirit," said Sir John. And he hesitated to proceed.

"What have they done?" cried the Archbishop. "Fear not to tell me."

"They have put to death your seneschal, Siward, because he bravely refused to deliver up the palace to them," replied Sir John.

"Heaven's vengeance will light upon them for the bloody deed!" ejaculated the Archbishop.

"Had your Grace been there, I doubt not you would have fallen a victim to their vengeful rage," continued Sir John.

"They shall be terribly requited!" cried Richard, fiercely. "We will march upon them at once, with all the force we can muster."

"The enterprise is too perilous to be attempted, my gracious liege," replied Sir John Holland, gravely. "So numerous are the rebels, that they would overpower any force you could bring against them. Canterbury, as I have just stated, is in revolt. The insurgents have compelled the Mayor and aldermen to swear fidelity to their cause; and if any of the burghers continue loyal, they dare not declare themselves. Many gentlemen have taken refuge in the monasteries and religious houses; but even there they are scarcely safe from these vile and bloodthirsty miscreants. If your

Majesty seeks to punish them, you must needs besiege the city, for they will hold out against you."

"Alas! that it should be so!" exclaimed the Archbishop. "'Tis woful that those whom I have nourished as children, should act thus."

"The city will be speedily recovered," said Sir Simon Burley. "But no rash attempt must be made against it, or the result will be disastrous."

"That is certain," observed Sir John. "As yet, I have only spoken of Canterbury; but every town in Kent, every village, is in a state of revolt. Our journey hither has been attended with the greatest risk. Do I exaggerate, Sir Osbert?"

"Not in the least, my good lord!" replied the knight appealed to. "I can add my testimony to your own. We were compelled to avoid Rochester and all the large towns on our way, and even the inhabitants of the little villages tried to stop us. Had we not travelled by night, we should not have arrived here safely."

"You give a fearful picture, but I doubt not a truthful one," said the Archbishop. "This insurrection seems to have spread with the rapidity of a devouring flame."

"No wonder, since the combustibles have been everywhere prepared," observed Sir Simon. "Who are the leaders of the rebellion?" he added, to Sir John Holland.

"The ostensible leaders are Wat Tyler, the smith of Dartford; an outlaw, who calls himself Jack Straw; and a friar named John Ball, whom it would have been well if his Grace of Canterbury had hanged. 'Tis suspected there are some great persons, by whom the outbreak has been contrived, and who secretly direct the rebels."

"Have those great persons been named?" asked the King.

"My liege, it is said—falsely, no doubt—that your uncles are concerned in the plot," replied Sir John Holland.

"We have already heard as much, but are loth to believe it," replied Richard.

"I grieve to say that the rumour that the Duke of Lancaster hath had a hand in the plot is generally credited by the insurgents themselves."

"Then Sir John Philpot was right!" cried the King. "'Tis clear our uncle's name supports the rebel cause."

"Believe it not, my liege," cried Chaucer.

"How! is my word doubted?" exclaimed Sir John Holland.

"No, my lord," replied Chaucer. "But you have been misinformed."

"I crave a moment's hearing, my liege," said the Baron de Vertain, who had hitherto taken no part in the discussion. "Before your Majesty comes to a decision as to the course to be pursued at this crisis, I beseech you to weigh well the consequences of allowing the rebels to march towards London unchecked. For all the excesses they may commit, your Majesty and your Ministers will be held responsible—and justly so, in my opinion. At all hazards, the rebellious rout ought to be stopped, and a heavy blow inflicted upon them."

"How is it to be inflicted, and by whom?" asked Richard.

"Sir John Philpot has asked for two thousand men," replied the Baron. "Give me two hundred, and I will make the attempt. But no time must be lost."

"On my return to the Tower, I will ascertain the number of the garrison, and if I can spare two hundred men, you shall have them, my liege," observed Sir John Burley.

"I will not be outdone, Baron!" cried Sir John Philpot. "I will find two hundred hardy companions, and will go with you."

"You will both be slain," remarked Sir Simon.

"What matter, if we check this rabble?" cried Philpot. "We shall die in a good cause, and our example will animate others."

Though some further discussion ensued, no change was made in the arrangements proposed by Sir Simon Burley, which were approved by the rest of the Council, and by the Princess.

It was therefore decided that the King should keep his Court, for the present, at the Tower. The Princess, however, determined to remain at Eltham till further tidings should be received of the rebels.

The royal party then adjourned to the banqueting-hall, where a sumptuous repast awaited them.

X.

THE LIEUTENANT OF THE TOWER.

AFTER taking leave of his mother, Richard set out for the Tower with a large retinue. He was accompanied by the Archbishop of Canterbury, the Lord of St. John's, Sir Simon Burley, Baron de Vertain, the Lord Mayor, Sir John Philpot, Chaucer, and Messer Benedetto.

Sir Eustace de Valletort remained with the Princess, to act for her in case of any sudden emergency.

It has been mentioned that the Lord Mayor had brought with him a numerous escort. These men-at-arms served as a guard to the King—part of them riding in front of the royal *cortége*, and part in the rear.

As Richard crossed London Bridge, trumpets were blown at the gates, and many persons came forth to look at the procession; but no shouts were uttered, and the people generally appeared sullen and discontented.

Nor did his Majesty meet with a better reception as he rode along Thames Street, though he proceeded at a slow pace, and bowed graciously to the concourse.

Much mortified, Richard made some observations on the moody looks of the people to the Archbishop, who replied—

"Their demeanour proves they are as disaffected as we have been told, my liege. The affections of your people have been alienated from you by those who have designs upon your throne. The spirit of rebellion is abroad, and must be extinguished."

Highly indignant at the insolent and unbecoming deportment of the populace, the

Lord Mayor escorted the King to the Bulwark Gate of the Tower, and there quitted him with the strongest expressions of loyalty and devotion.

"I shall always be close at hand," he said; "always ready to fly to your Majesty, in case of need."

"Enough!" cried Richard: "I never doubted Sir William Walworth's loyalty. If all others fail me, he will not."

Messer Benedetto departed at the same time, and, in taking leave of the King, said that if his Majesty should require money, all his own funds and those of his partners should be at his disposal.

Richard thanked him heartily, but trusted he should not need a loan.

"Nay, my liege," replied the Lombard merchant; "'tis not as a loan that I offer the money, but as a subsidy."

"By our Lady! you are a true man,

Messer Benedetto!" exclaimed the King, well pleased. "We trust we shall not have to apply to you; but be sure we shall not forget your noble offer."

Sir John Philpot entered the Tower with the King, to await his Majesty's decision as to the proposed attack on the rebels.

A feeling of dejection, caused by the cold reception he had met with, had taken possession of the young monarch; but this was quickly dispelled as he crossed the moat and rode through the wide arch of the By-ward Tower, amid the bruit of clarions and the beating of drums.

The outer ward was lined with archers, arbalestriers, and piquiers, in their full accoutrements, and making a goodly show.

The sight of these hardy men, who regarded him with loyal looks, raised Richard's confidence, and he felt assured that while they and their comrades continued faithful, his crown could not be wrested from him.

At that time the Tower contained within its limits a royal palace of considerable size, situated at the south of the White Tower, and occupying the whole of the space between that majestic structure and the inner walls.

The palace was approached by a gateway flanked by towers, leading into a small court, and here Richard and his attendants alighted.

His Majesty was received by Sir Nicholas Bonde, the Lieutenant of the Tower, Sir Robert de Namur, the Baron de Gommegines, Sir Henry de Sauselles, and some others.

While the Archbishop of Canterbury, the Lord of St. John's, and Chaucer entered the palace, the King addressed himself at once to the Lieutenant, and said—

"Sir Nicholas, we desire to send a small party of men against the rebels."

"Under whose command, my liege?" inquired the Lieutenant, bowing.

"Under the joint command of the Baron de Vertain and Sir John Philpot," replied Richard. "Can they have two hundred archers?"

"No, my liege; but if they could, what would such a trifling force as that avail against the rebel host?"

"Leave that to us, Sir Nicholas," interposed Philpot. "Give us a hundred archers and we will bring back Wat Tyler's head."

"If you will engage to do that, you shall have them and welcome, Sir John," rejoined the Lieutenant, with a grim smile.

"If I do not you shall have my own, Sir Nicholas," cried Philpot.

"Nay, by my troth! I want it not," said the Lieutenant. "But I suppose your request must be granted, though the fortress will be denuded of a third of the garrison."

"Heed not that, Sir Nicholas," observed the King. "Let the men be got ready forthwith."

"A hundred, sire—not one more," said the Lieutenant.

"But you have promised to bring another hundred, Sir John?" observed De Vertain.

"And I will keep my word," rejoined Philpot. "Two hours hence, five score hardy companions, completely armed and well mounted, shall be on Tower Hill."

"And I will answer that the Baron de Vertain shall not keep you waiting," said Richard, glancing at the Lieutenant, who bowed in assent.

"When next I appear before your Majesty, I trust to bring you good news," said Philpot.

"Would I could go with you!" cried the King. "But it seems that must not be."

"Nay, my gracious liege; you are best here," said Sir John Philpot.

And, with a profound obeisance, he departed.

At the appointed hour, ten score armed horsemen appeared on Tower Hill.

Their leader, mounted on a powerful war-horse, protected by a chanfron and flanchières, wore a suit of ringed mail, closely fitting his limbs, and a hood of chain mail, that only left his face visible.

Over his armour he had a white surcoat, worked with his crest. The troop had a banner and pennons.

Almost at the same moment a company of well-mounted archers, numbering likewise two hundred, and commanded by a noble knight, sheathed in complete mail, and riding a richly-caparisoned charger, crossed the moat, with a broad banner borne before them and pennons flying.

A loud shout was raised by the party on the Hill, which was responded to by the archers.

The two companies then formed a junction, and rode off at a quick pace towards London Bridge, causing much wonderment and speculation among the citizens as they proceeded.

From the eastern battlements of the Tower Richard witnessed their departure.

As they disappeared, he heaved a sigh.

His Majesty was attended by the Lieutenant, Sir Simon Burley, and the Baron de Gommegines, none of whom seemed hopeful.

" 'Tis the maddest expedition ever planned," observed Sir Simon. "We shall see none of them again. Worst of all, your Majesty will lose two hundred archers and ten score stout men-of-arms, of whom you are sorely in need."

XI.

SIR EUSTACE DE VALLETORT MAKES A DISCLOSURE TO EDITHA.

THOUGH not free from alarm, the Princess of Wales deemed herself safe at Eltham under the care of a commander so vigilant and experienced as Sir Eustace de Valletort, and if an attack upon the palace should be threatened, she knew she could easily retreat to the Tower.

Delighted with her new position, Editha had felt quite happy until the arrival of Sir John Holland at the palace; but his presence, though disagreeable, gave her little uneasiness, because she could rely upon the Princess's protection.

Sir John was greatly surprised to find the young damsel among his mother's attendants, but he asked no questions, and gave no sign that he even recognised her. That he had abandoned his designs cannot be asserted, but he masked them under an air of haughtiness and indifference.

But there was a person at the palace who excited a very different feeling in Editha's bosom from that she experienced towards the young noble.

From the first moment she beheld Sir Eustace de Valletort, she had felt an interest in him for which she could in no wise account. She was attracted towards him as if by a spell.

A similar sympathetic feeling—though perhaps even stronger—had been experienced by Sir Eustace. Mingled emotions agitated his breast when he gazed upon her, and carefully perused her features. He had arrived at a certain conclusion respecting her, even before his surmises were confirmed by his discourse with the Princess.

No opportunity of addressing her in private occurred until after the departure of the young King and his retinue for the Tower. The facility for the interview he so ardently desired was afforded by the Princess, who sent Editha with a message to him.

He was in the garden at the time, alone, pacing to and fro on the terrace, musing sadly on the past.

When the young damsel came forth, he advanced to meet her, showing by his manner how pleased he was to see her.

After she had delivered her message, which was of little import, and did not require an answer, she was about to retire, but Sir Eustace detained her.

"Stay, fair damsel," he said; "I would fain have a word with you."

Predisposed towards him, as we have described her, Editha very willingly complied.

"You will not wonder at the interest I take in you when I tell you that you resemble one who was very dear to me, and is now lost to me for ever."

Having said thus much in accents that betrayed deep emotion, he paused.

Editha did not venture to make an observation.

Presently he continued—

"Yes, you are very like her—so much so, that I could almost have declared you are her daughter."

"But the Princess has acquainted you with my story, noble sir," cried Editha, trembling. "You know that I am——"

"I know that you are not the daughter

of those who have brought you up," said Sir Eustace.

Editha gazed at him in astonishment, scarcely able to believe she had heard aright.

"You look too good—too kind to trifle with me, noble sir," she cried. "Is this true? Speak—in pity, speak!"

And she clasped his hand in her agitation.

"It is true! I swear it before heaven!" he rejoined, solemnly.

Editha had become pale as death, but she maintained her self-possession by a powerful effort.

"I will open my heart to you, noble sir," she said, in low, tremulous tones, "as I would to my confessor. At times, this conviction has forced itself upon me, but I have always dismissed it, and blamed myself for indulging it."

After a momentary pause, she added, earnestly, "'Tis an inexpressible relief to find I am not Wat Tyler's daughter. Though I am beholden to him for much kindness, and he has ever treated me as a father, I cannot love him as I once did."

"I do not wonder at it," said Sir Eustace. "'Tis proper, therefore, this disclosure should be made to you. Think of him no more."

"Nay, I must needs think of him," she said, "unless the past can be obliterated. But you have more to tell me."

"Be content with what you have already learnt," replied Sir Eustace, gravely. "I have no authority to make any further disclosure."

"Do you lack authority?" she cried.

"Yes," he rejoined. "There are secrets that cannot be revealed save by dying lips—perchance not even then. Question me no more. You cannot doubt that I am deeply interested in you?"

"No, no! Your looks proclaim your sincerity!" she cried.

"I will prove it to you," he said, in accents that vibrated to her heart. "Since I cannot name your father—since you may never behold him—I will take his place. I will be a father to you!"

With a look of indescribable gratitude, she seized his hand and pressed it to her lips. At the same time she made an effort to kneel, but he prevented her.

"Control yourself, my child," he said, with a look of tenderest affection; "we may be observed."

The apprehension was justified. The terrace on which they stood faced the state apartments; and from an open window in the great gallery Sir John Holland and Sir Osbert Montacute witnessed the interview just described.

Entirely misconstruing the nature of the meeting, and influenced by jealousy, the young noble vowed revenge.

"This coy damsel is a good specimen of her fickle sex!" observed Sir John. "She regards me with aversion, and flies from me, yet she rushes into the arms of a man old enough to be her father! 'Tis intolerable! Sir Eustace may plume himself on his conquest; but he shall not boast long, for, by St. Paul! I will rob him of his prize! But see, they separate; though she seems as if she could scarcely tear herself away, and casts a tender look back at him Let us intercept her!"

With this he hastily quitted the window, and, followed by Sir Osbert, hurried to the entrance-hall, through which he thought it likely Editha would pass.

And so it turned out, for, just as they reached it, the young damsel came in.

On seeing Sir John, she tried to avoid him, but he stopped her.

"Why so cold and distant to me, fair damsel?" he said. "You can bestow sweet smiles and soft words on others."

"Let me pass, I pray you, my lord," she said. "I am going to the Princess."

But he detained her while he said, in a low voice—

"Assume this manner, if you choose, to others, but it will not impose on me. I saw what took place on the terrace not many minutes ago. You were not reserved with Sir Eustace de Valletort. Ah! I have called a blush to your cheeks."

"Sir Eustace will know how to answer you, my lord!" she rejoined, proudly.

"I shall not trouble myself with him," he returned. "Had you not better purchase my silence with the Princess?"

"How, my lord? Do you dare to insinuate——"

"Nay; I shall insinuate nothing. I shall merely mention to her Grace what Sir Osbert and myself beheld from the gallery window. Ha! you tremble now and turn pale!"

"This conduct is unworthy of you, my lord," she cried; "but I am well assured Sir Eustace will resent the imputation you have cast upon him! Let me go!"

Sir John, however, might have persisted in the annoyance, had not an interruption occurred that compelled him to release her.

From the door communicating with the court, two knights entered the hall.

They were the Baron de Vertain and Sir John Philpot, who had called at the palace in the hope of inducing Sir John Holland and some of his attendants to accompany them on their expedition.

On beholding them, the young noble quickly released Editha; and hurrying away, she ascended the great staircase, and proceeded to the Princess's private apartments.

"I did not expect to see you back so soon," cried Sir John, addressing the new comers.

De Vertain then explained their errand; and, after a brief consultation with Sir Osbert, the young noble agreed to go with them.

"If we can slay their leaders, we shall strike terror into the host," he said. "We must dash upon them like falcons on their prey, and, having struck down those we aim at, beat a hasty retreat. Where are your men?"

"In the park," replied De Vertain. "Will you return with us?"

"In half an hour I shall be ready with

my followers," replied Sir John. "Will you wait so long?"

"Gladly," replied the two knights.

How they passed the interval it boots not to relate. They did not see the Princess, but had some converse with Sir Eustace de Valletort, who came into the hall.

In less time than he had mentioned, Sir John Holland had donned his armour and mounted his charger. A dozen young nobles, as many knights and esquires, and a score of armed men, were likewise ready to attend him.

He then rode forth from the palace, with De Vertain and Sir John Philpot, who complimented him upon his extraordinary promptitude.

They found the two companies waiting for them in the avenue; and the whole party set off in good spirits for Rochester, where they expected to encounter the insurgents.

XII.

HOW SIR JOHN HOLLAND RETURNED FROM THE EXPEDITION.

FOR two days no tidings were heard of the expedition, either at the Tower or at Eltham. Nor was any reliable intelligence received of the proceedings of the rebels. It was rumoured that the latter had quitted Canterbury, that their numbers had enormously increased, and that they were marching on Rochester, committing terrible excesses on the way; but nothing certain was known.

Great anxiety was felt by the Princess for her son, Sir John Holland. He did not take leave of her before he set out, well knowing she would oppose his departure;

but he left a message for her, saying he should soon be back. But he came not, and she had little expectation of seeing him again.

That his absence was not regretted by Editha need scarcely be said; and her chief fear was that he would speedily return.

Apprehensions of a very different kind were felt by Sir Eustace de Valletort. He did not anticipate that the expedition would be successful, and had not encouraged it. Well knowing Sir John Holland's obstinacy of character, he did not remonstrate with him at taking away so many armed men, but he was much vexed to lose them.

Though the force now at Sir Eustace's command was insufficient for the defence of the palace, he made every possible preparation for the attack he had reason to apprehend, and neglected no precaution against a sudden surprise. Both drawbridges were kept constantly raised; the gates were strongly guarded, and sentinels stationed in the turrets of the battlemented walls.

But for two days, as we have said, all remained tranquil, and no tidings were received either of friends or enemies.

During this interval, no word in private had been exchanged between Sir Eustace and Editha, and they had only met when she was in attendance in the banqueting-hall or elsewhere.

Evidently, the knight put great constraint upon himself; but he could not hide—at least, not from the quick eye of the Princess—the deep interest he felt in the young damsel.

As to Editha, ever since the interview on the terrace, an extraordinary change had taken place in her breast. With the intuitive perception of her sex, and by putting many circumstances together, she had been able to penetrate the mystery that had surrounded her.

Nothing doubting that Sir Eustace was her father, she had already begun to feel for him the affection of a daughter. Happily, she could indulge these feelings without being distracted by the presence of Sir John Holland.

The Princess sought for no explanation. She divined the truth. But, despite her anxieties for the King, for Sir John Holland, and even for herself, her thoughts were much occupied about the young damsel.

It was, indeed, a most anxious period, for no one could tell what the next few days might bring forth.

Gloom settled upon the palace. All its inmates, even the youngest and most lighthearted, seemed oppressed by forebodings of ill. Mirth and festivity were completely banished—even from the great kitchen where the household were wont to assemble, and where laughter had always heretofore resounded over the cups of strong ale and mead at supper.

Extremely devout, as we have shown, the Princess passed much of her time in prayer, and was much more frequently in the chapel, attending the performance of religious rites, than in the hall.

On these occasions, Editha was always with her—and indeed, so were her ladies.

Thus the time passed at the palace.

Late in the afternoon of the third day, the guard on the summit of the northern gateway descried a small party of horsemen coming along the avenue.

Steeds and riders looked wearied and distressed, and the former seemed ready to drop with fatigue. To reach the palace would be as much as they could achieve.

No doubt this little troop was the remnant of the companies that had set forth so valiantly to check the rebels.

Word being sent to Sir Eustace of the approach of the party, he ordered the drawbridge to be instantly lowered, and went forth to meet them.

Sir John Holland could now be plainly distinguished, with his armour battered and blood-stained; but neither Sir John Philpot nor the Baron de Vertain were to be seen.

When the young noble dismounted, his steed shook as if it would have fallen, and he himself could scarcely stand.

"I am sorry to see you thus, my lord," said Sir Eustace, supporting him. "I trust you are not badly hurt?"

"No," replied Sir John, with a ghastly smile, and in a hoarse voice. "I got a few scratches in the encounter with the rebels—but nothing to signify."

"That is well," rejoined Sir Eustace. "But I do not see De Vertain and Philpot. What of them?" he added, in an anxious tone.

"If they have escaped with life as I have done, 'tis the best that has befallen them!" replied Sir John. "But I have seen nothing of them since the fight. We were worsted by the rabble. But we have done some execution upon them," he added, with a grim smile.

He then became exceedingly faint, and Sir Eustace besought him to enter the palace, and fortify himself with a cordial.

"While I am able to speak," said the young noble, faintly, "let me state that I am pursued by a large party of rebels. We owe our escape from them entirely to the swiftness of our horses."

"Are they far off?" demanded Sir Eustace, anxiously.

"Some five or six miles, it may be," replied Sir John Holland. "The troop, which numbers several hundred men, is led by the outlaw styling himself Jack Straw—a desperate and daring villain, who has conceived a deadly animosity against me. With him is a certain Conrad Basset—a young man of courage and enterprise, with whom I have had a personal conflict, and I should have slain him if it had not been for the Outlaw."

"Then you believe this rebel leader is in pursuit of you, my lord?" observed Sir Eustace.

"I am sure of it," replied Sir John. "And I am also sure he will attack the palace when he finds I am here. He has vowed to capture me, or slay me, and he will try to keep his word."

"Then tarry here no longer, but come within," cried Sir Eustace.

As they moved slowly towards the palace, they were followed by the men-at-arms, who looked quite as much exhausted as their leader.

When all had crossed the drawbridge, Sir Eustace gave orders that it should be raised, the gates shut, and a sharp look-out kept by the sentinels.

XIII.

SIR JOHN HOLLAND'S NARRATIVE.

NOT without difficulty did Sir John Holland reach the banqueting-hall; but, after emptying a goblet of wine, he felt much revived, and was able to converse with the Princess, who on hearing of his return, had flown to meet him, full of maternal solicitude.

In reply to her inquiries, Sir John said that the expedition he had joined proceeded to the hills above Rochester, which they found occupied by the rebels.

"They are in great force," he continued; "and we ascertained that they now number sixty thousand men—perhaps more. They are besieging Rochester Castle, and I much fear will take it. Since nothing could be done against such a numerous host, we waited on the hills till this morning, when we perceived a large troop of horse come forth from the city. They were in marching order, and must have numbered six hundred at the least. Their leaders were the Outlaw and Conrad Basset. Though our force was so disproportionate, we did not hesitate to attack them. Dashing upon them suddenly, we caused great slaughter, killing them in heaps. We had hoped to rout them, but they held their ground, and, in the conflict that ensued, being overpowered by numbers, nearly all our men were slain. My aim was to kill the two leaders; but while I was engaged with Conrad Basset, the Outlaw joined him, and I was forced to fly, bringing with me only a dozen men. As you may well believe, we had to ride hard, or we should have been captured. For some miles the Outlaw was close behind us, but though he was well mounted, his men were not, and he could not come on alone. So we soon left them at a distance. But they have not abandoned the pursuit. We shall have them here anon."

Just as Sir John had brought his narrative to an end, and his mother, who had listened to it with breathless interest, was beginning to question him as to his companions-in-arms, a great noise was heard without, followed by joyful shouts, with which the names of De Vertain, Philpot, and Sir Osbert Montacute were mingled.

"Ha! by St. Paul! they are safe—they are here!" cried the young noble, starting to his feet.

Next moment Sir Eustace de Valletort entered the hall, bringing with him the three valiant personages in question.

They looked greatly fatigued, and had

all suffered more or less in the encounter with the rebels.

Such greetings passed between them and Sir John Holland as can only be exchanged under similar circumstances.

Very few words sufficed to explain the manner of their escape.

All three had been unhorsed—or rather, their horses had been killed by the rebels; but each had caught a fresh steed, and had managed to extricate himself from the hostile throng by hewing down or trampling upon all who sought to stay him.

Once free, they had joined together; when, learning from the shouts that Sir John Holland had escaped, they had followed him as fast as they could, but must have taken a different route to Eltham.

"Heaven be thanked, you are safe!" exclaimed the Princess.

"We have accomplished nothing," said

Sir John Philpot; "for though we have slain many rebels, we have lost nearly all our men, and have failed in our chief design. But your Grace must not remain here. The rebels are at our heels, and most assuredly will attack the palace."

"The Princess need be under no apprehension," said Sir Eustace de Valletort. "An underground passage leads from the palace to the hunting-tower above Greenwich, by which she can safely depart at any time with her ladies and an escort. As you know, there is always a royal barge at Greenwich."

"I have heard of such a subterranean passage as you describe, but have never seen it," said the Princess.

"The entrance to the passage is secret, madam, but I am acquainted with it," replied Sir Eustace, "and will conduct you to it whenever you desire."

"I will wait to see what happens," said the Princess.

"You had best not wait too long, madam," observed Sir John Holland.

At this juncture an esquire entered the hall.

"Methinks we shall learn something now that may influence your Grace's decision," said Sir Eustace. "Hast thou aught to say to me?" he added, to the esquire.

"A large body of horsemen have just appeared," was the reply. "As far as I can guess, they are about six hundred strong—half being archers, and half crossbowmen. They have halted at the further end of the avenue. I must not omit to mention that they have a banner of St. George with them, and half a dozen pennons."

"Ha! the insolent villains!" exclaimed Sir Eustace.

Just then, a second esquire entered the hall, and stated that a herald, attended by a trumpeter, was riding slowly towards the palace gate.

"A herald! Ha!" ejaculated Sir Eustace. " I will hear what he has to say."

"I will go with you, Sir Eustace," said the Princess. " I shall be guided as to my departure by what takes place."

"We will all go !" cried Sir John Holland. " Lend me your arm, Baron," he added, to De Vertain.

The Princess was then conducted by Sir Eustace to the battlemented walls adjoining the gate.

XIV.

CONRAD BASSET DEMANDS THAT SIR JOHN HOLLAND SHALL BE DELIVERED UP.

ON gaining this position, they saw the herald, preceded by a trumpeter, arrayed in a tabard, riding slowly along the avenue.

He was well mounted, and well armed; and, as he drew nearer, the Princess was struck by his proud looks and deportment.

"That man cannot be a peasant," she remarked.

"'Tis Conrad Basset," replied Sir John Holland.

When he got within fifty yards of the gateway, the herald halted, and the trumpeter, who was a little in advance, sounded his horn thrice.

As the ringing notes died away, an officer, stationed with a guard of archers, on the summit of the barbacan, called out, in a loud voice—

"What wouldst thou?"

Without betraying the slightest fear, or abating the haughtiness of his deportment, the herald rode towards the barbacan, and spoke thus, in a clear voice, and with great deliberation :—

"Say to the noble, or knight, who may be in command of the palace, that we, the commons of Kent, having been outrageously treated by Sir John Holland, half-brother to the King, who hath endeavoured to carry off a damsel by force from her father, and well knowing that we shall not obtain justice in any other manner, demand the delivery up to us of the said knight, in order that he may be punished summarily for his offence."

Astounded by the demand, Sir John Holland's pallid cheek flushed darkly, and he would have instantly and furiously responded if the Princess had not checked him.

The rejoinder, however, was given in a stern, determined tone by Sir Eustace.

"Tell those who have sent thee," said the commander, "that I, Sir Eustace de Valletort, now in charge of this palace, and representing her Highness the Princess of Wales, treat their insolent demand with scorn. Nor, were it even couched in befitting language, would I vouchsafe to listen to it. I will not treat with rebels, nor have I any authority for what I am about to say; yet, having some pity for thy misguided companions, I would have thee repeat my words to them. If they desire to obtain certain liberties and privileges, they must at once lay down their arms, and return to their allegiance to their sovereign lord, the King."

To this address the herald returned a contemptuous laugh.

"Since you refuse to deliver up Sir John Holland," he said, in the same haughty and defiant tone as before, "we will take him, and behead him!"

So wroth was the young noble at this audacious announcement, that he would have ordered the archers to bend their bows upon the speaker, if Sir Eustace had not interposed.

"Hold!" he exclaimed, authoritatively. "No harm must be done him."

The herald seemed to feel secure, for after calmly surveying the battlements, he turned his horse's head, and rode slowly back.

Ere long he was joined by a horseman,

who galloped from the rebel host to meet him, and was recognised by several of the lookers-on as the Outlaw Chief.

After a few words had passed between the pair, the Outlaw turned partly round, and shook his hand menacingly at the barbacan.

Having witnessed this ominous meeting, the Princess quitted the battlements, and returned to the banqueting-hall, where a conference took place, at which Sir Eustace and the rest of the knights assisted.

All were of opinion that she should set forth for the Tower without delay.

"A few hours hence," urged Sir Eustace, "flight may be impossible. Now it can be safely accomplished."

"Say no more, Sir Eustace," she rejoined. "I will prepare for my departure at once. You must escort me, my lord," she added, to Sir John Holland.

"Were I to quit the palace at this juncture, madam," he replied, "the rebels would say I feared them. They shall both see me and feel the weight of my arm."

"Beware how you fall into their hands, my son," she remarked, anxiously. "They will not spare you. You had better come with me."

"Sir Osbert Montacute will escort you, madam—*I* cannot," said Sir John.

On this intimation, Sir Osbert instantly proffered his services, which were graciously accepted by the Princess, though she cast a reproachful look at her son.

"By the time your preparations are made, madam, all shall be ready for you," said Sir Eustace. "I counsel you to take your jewels and valuables with you."

The Princess then withdrew to her own

apartment, from which, in less than half an hour, she reappeared with her ladies, each of whom had a casket in her hand.

Amongst them was Editha.

Meanwhile, by Sir Eustace's orders, all the Princess's personal attendants, pages and others, had assembled in the hall. With them were her confessor, her almoner, and her physician. Besides these, there were half a dozen armed attendants.

Sir Eustace and Sir Osbert were waiting for her, but she did not see her son or Sir John Philpot.

"Sir John Holland is on the ramparts, madam," observed De Vertain. "He charged me to say that he hoped soon to join you at the Tower."

"Has the assault commenced?" inquired the Princess, alarmed by the sounds that reached her ear.

"It has, madam," replied Sir Eustace. "Will it please you to come with me? The entrance to the subterranean passage is on the other side of the court. All is ready for your departure."

XV.

THE SUBTERRANEAN PASSAGE.

AS the party traversed the court, shouts and other noises could be distinctly heard; and as Sir Eustace's looks plainly showed that he longed to be at his post, the Princess quickened her pace.

In another moment they reached a tower at the lower end of the quadrangle, and, passing through an arched doorway guarded by a couple of halberdiers, entered a circular chamber on the ground-floor.

In the centre of this chamber, which had an arched and groined roof, and was lighted by narrow loopholed windows, was a trap-door, now lying open.

The trap-door was of unusual size, and communicated with an underground chamber, from which ran the subterranean passage about to be tracked by the fugitives.

The vault was illumined by torches borne by men-at-arms.

"Having brought your Grace thus far," said Sir Eustace, "I will now commit you to the care of Sir Osbert Montacute, who has full instructions. I trust your Grace will arrive safely at the Tower."

With a valedictory look, full of tenderness, at Editha, he then hurried off to the ramparts.

The underground chamber to which the fugitives descended was of considerable size, and solidly constructed of stone.

In a few minutes all had come down, and the trap-door was closed and fastened.

Before proceeding, the Princess called

Editha to her, and bade her keep by her side.

The word being given by Sir Osbert Montacute, who marched a little in advance of the Princess, the whole party entered the subterranean passage, which was sufficiently wide and lofty, well built with brick, and arched throughout.

At first, it was perfectly dry, though further on, as they passed under the moat, the atmosphere became humid.

The torch-bearers moved on in front, and, seen by this light, the procession formed a very striking picture.

Some of the Court damsels manifested alarm, but the greater part of them talked and laughed lightly, as did the pages. The confessor, who was close behind the Princess, said never a word, and Editha remained silent.

By-and-by they came to a strong iron

gate, which had to be unlocked, and some forty yards further on there was another gate.

The party were now under the moat, and the great chillness caused a general shivering among the damsels; but after they had passed through the second gate the dampness ceased.

Infinite care had been bestowed upon the construction of this remarkable subterranean passage, some portion of which still exists. Not only were the walls strongly built, as described, but air was admitted by singularly contrived shafts. There were also branch passages, stairs, and decoys, intended to lure a hostile party to pitfalls.

These avenues to destruction were pointed out to the Princess, and their purposes explained to her by Sir Osbert Montacute; and she shuddered as she gazed into the dark passages.

"We cannot miss our way in this mysterious labyrinth?" she inquired, in an anxious whisper, of Sir Osbert.

"Impossible!" he rejoined. "Our guide, Baldwin, is familiar with the place."

Other passages were next pointed out connected with sally-ports, and Sir Osbert thought these might possibly now be used in an attack upon the besiegers.

That Editha was without alarm, we will not venture to assert; but she exhibited no sign of trepidation, and surprised the Princess by her firmness. However, her courage was put to a much more severe test anon.

The party had proceeded without hindrance of any kind, and with tolerable expedition, for about a quarter of a mile, when Baldwin, the torch bearer, who acted as guide, and was a little in advance of the others, suddenly stopped, and held up his hand in a warning manner.

At this signal, those who followed stopped likewise.

"In heaven's name! what is the matter?" cried the Princess, in great alarm, which was shared by all those near her.

"The enemy is in the passage, madam," rejoined Sir Osbert, with forced calmness. "Hear you not those sounds?"

And as he spoke, sounds of an approaching party were heard in the distance.

"They appear to be numerous," he continued. "'Tis well for us they have betrayed themselves. Had they come on cautiously, we must have fallen into their hands. Extinguish the torches," he added to the men in advance.

The order was instantly obeyed, and the passage plunged in profound darkness.

Half-stifled cries arose from the terrified

damsels; but they quickly became quiet, conscious that their safety depended on silence.

By this time Sir Osbert had been joined by Baldwin.

"We must instantly turn back, my lord," said the man. "We shall not be able to reach the gates; but I will take you to a retreat where her Grace and her ladies may be concealed."

"You hear what he says, madam," remarked Sir Osbert. "Will you trust him?"

"I will," she replied; "I do not doubt his fidelity."

"Come with me, then, madam," cried Baldwin, making his way through the throng, while the Princess followed, grasping Editha's hand.

Close behind them came the rest of the party, whose movements were quickened by sounds proclaiming that the enemy was drawing nearer.

A side passage, however, was soon reached, and the whole party being safely bestowed within it, Sir Osbert, with Baldwin and the armed men, stationed themselves near the entrance.

They were less apprenhensive of discovery, since it was certain that the rebels, who were now close at hand, had not got torches.

Nor did the villanous intruders appear to be aware that they had accidentally interfered with the Princess's flight. Their object seemed to be to obtain access to the palace by means of the subterranean passage, the existence of which had doubtless been revealed to them by some traitor.

As they were passing along in the darkness, one of them chanced to put out his hand, and detected the side passage wherein the fugitives had taken refuge, and immediately called out to his comrades—

"Hold! you are going wrong."

"How knowst thou that, Elias Liripipe? for I guess 'tis thou by thy voice, though I cannot see thee," rejoined the leader.

"Yes, 'tis I, Captain Hothbrand," replied Liripipe. "This is the right way."

"Methinks thou art mistaken," said Hothbrand. "But, prithee, examine the passage as well as thou canst."

"I will proceed along it to a short distance," replied Liripipe.

He had not gone far, however, when he roared out suddenly, "Help! help!" and rushed back as quickly as he could.

"What is the matter?" demanded Hothbrand.

"I have received a blow on the head that well-nigh stunned me," replied Liripipe.

"Didst hear any one move?"

"I cannot say I did. The blow was sudden and violent."

"Bah! 'tis mere fancy. Thou hast knocked thy head against the wall," cried Hothbrand. "Come along."

And the rebel band marched on, greatly to the relief of those inside the passage.

As soon as the enemy was out of hearing, the fugitives came forth, and again pursued their onward course.

Though deprived of the torchlight, they proceeded far more expeditiously than heretofore, their fears accelerating their movements. The fugitives had every reason to apprehend the speedy return of the rebels, as they knew the latter would be stopped by the iron gates.

Another ground of apprehension existed, and this was that the outlet of the subterranean passage might be watched by the enemy.

Such, however, did not prove to be the case. In the small hunting-tower in Greenwich Park, in the lower storey of which the fugitives came forth from their underground journey, no one was to be seen but the persons in charge of the building.

These persons declared that no rebels had been seen near the building, nor could they comprehend how any hostile intruders could have found access to the passage. Certainly, it must have been elsewhere, and not from the vaults beneath the tower.

Apparently the Princess was satisfied with the explanation, though credence was not attached to it by Sir Osbert Montacute, who could not comprehend from what other point the passage could have been entered; and Baldwin, who was better informed than any one else, entertained the same opinion.

The Princess did not remain long at the hunting-tower; but descended from the woody heights on which it was situated, to Greenwich, where the royal barge was moored.

Rejoicing at her escape, she went on board with her attendants, and gave orders that the oarsmen should proceed at once to the Tower.

As the gilded bark, propelled by twenty stout rowers, clad in the royal livery, cut its way through the then clear and beautiful river, the Princess gradually recovered her spirits, which had been sadly shaken by her perilous journey from the palace of Eltham.

Before entering the barge, her Grace, having no further occasion for an escort, dismissed Sir Osbert Montacute and all the men-at-arms.

The gallant young knight expressed his intention of returning to the palace, at all hazards, through the subterranean passage. Unless the rebels should have found some other means of exit than by the fortified sallyport, he must needs encounter them, and would attack them. If he perished, it would be in a good cause.

With this bold resolve, Sir Osbert departed.

XVI.

HOW THE PRINCESS ARRIVED AT THE TOWER.

THE passage to the Tower in the splendid royal barge had all the charm of novelty to Editha, and the pleasant sensations awakened by the easy motion of the vessel, combined with the novelty of the various objects presented to her gaze, speedily put to flight the alarm and anxiety she had previously experienced.

The weather was delightful, and the contrast between the bright river, with the numerous barks floating upon it, and the sombre passages she had just tracked, was indeed striking. Besides, she was going to the Tower, the place of all others she most desired to visit. No wonder, therefore, that she quickly recovered her spirits.

As she neared the great city, her delight and wonder increased; but when at length the mighty bridge and the royal fortress burst upon her, she could scarcely control her emotions.

The Princess perceived from her looks what was passing in her mind, but made no remark, being greatly pre-occupied at the time.

For some minutes Editha's gaze had been fixed on the commanding White Tower, surmounted by the royal standard, and on the fortified towers around it; and thrilling sensations of awe and wonder were excited in her breast; but no sooner was the barge descried by the guard on St. Thomas's Tower, than trumpets were sounded loudly, and Sir Alan Murrieux, the Lieutenant, being informed that the Princess was approaching, hastened to the wharf with a large body of warders to receive her.

Before the Princess landed, Sir Simon Burley and the Baron de Gommegines had likewise reached the wharf, and the former gave her his hand as she stepped ashore.

"Your Grace is ever welcome at the Tower," said Sir Alan Murrieux, the Lieutenant, advancing to meet her; "but I much fear your present visit is not of your own choosing."

"You are right, good Sir Alan," she replied. "I know not whether the news has reached you that the Baron de Vertain, Sir John Philpot, and my son, Sir John Holland, have been discomfited by the rebels?"

"I grieve to hear it, madam," replied Sir Alan; "but we had little hope that the expedition would be successful."

"All are safe, I trust?" observed Sir Simon Burley, anxiously.

"They are all at Eltham," replied the Princess; "but they are still in some danger. They have been pursued by a large body of the insurgents, who are now besieging the palace. This is the cause of my sudden flight. As the palace is surrounded by the enemy, I could only escape, with my ladies, through the subterranean passage."

"Certes, you bring bad news, madam," said Sir Simon. "Some men-at-arms and archers must be sent to aid the besieged; yet I know not how it can be safely done."

"I am ready to take the command of any party you may send," observed De Gommegines.

"Men are wanting, my lord, not leaders," rejoined Sir Simon.

"The besiegers muster about five hundred, as I understand," observed the Princess. "They have archers and crossbowmen with them, and are under the command of the Outlaw Chief. Sir Eustace de Valletort has undertaken the defence of the palace."

"And better commander could not be found!" cried De Gommegines. "But he ought to have assistance. With a hundred lances these churls could be driven off!"

"Eltham palace shall never be taken by them, come what may!" cried Sir Simon.

"I am glad to hear you say that, Sir Simon!" cried the Princess.

By this time all the ladies, having disembarked, were now gathering round their royal mistress. They expressed the greatest satisfaction at having exchanged the doubtful security of Eltham for the protection of an impregnable fortress like the Tower.

"Here, at least, we are safe from the rebels!" cried the Lady Egelwine.

"I never liked the Tower half so much

as I do now," said the fair Agnes de Somerville. "I used to think it a dismal place; but, after the vaults of Eltham, it appears charming!"

"Did you observe how the deer in the park fled at the approach of the rebels?" remarked the dark-eyed Ela de Fauconberg. "They seemed to know that the leader was a deerstalker."

"I saw not the deer," replied the Lady Egelwine; "but I heard the ravens croak ominously."

"And I heard the bitterns boom," added the blonde Hawisia.

"And I saw several birds of prey, hawks and kites, hovering above the palace," said the lovely, but timorous, Sybilla de Feschamp.

"All these are portents of ill," said the Lady Egelwine. "I much fear the palace is doomed to destruction."

"Have no such fear, fair damsels," observed De Gommegines, who was standing by. " Eltham is not destined to become a den of robbers. When you return thither you will find the palace uninjured."

An exclamation, which Editha could not repress, attracted the Baron's attention, and he inquired her name.

The Lady Egelwine told him; adding, "She comes from the priory at Dartford, and is a great favourite of the Princess."

"So it appears," observed De Gommegines, as, in obedience to a sign, Editha took a place behind her royal mistress.

Meanwhile, Sir Simon Burley had quitted the Princess, in order to despatch a messenger with a letter to the Lord Mayor, telling him that Eltham was beleaguered by the rebels, and praying him to bring as many men-at-arms as he could without delay to succour the besieged.

It devolved, therefore, on the Lieutenant to conduct her Grace to St. Peter's Chapel in the White Tower, whither she desired to repair at once, to offer up thanks to Heaven for her Providential deliverance. Her confessor had already gone on to the chapel.

As the Princess and her train proceeded to the inner ward, Editha was enabled to take a rapid survey of certain portions of the ancient palatial fortress, and she was greatly impressed by the stern grandeur of the White Tower, which burst upon her after she had passed through the arched gateway of the Garden Tower, since known as the Bloody Tower.

Not being aware of the situation of St. Peter's Chapel, she was surprised when the Princess entered the massive donjon, and, ascending a spiral staircase, proceeded along a corridor to a door, before which stood a couple of halberdiers and an officer of the guard.

Here the Princess learnt that the King was then in the chapel, and that mass was being performed by the Archbishop of Canterbury.

Waiting for a moment till all her attendants had assembled, she entered the sacred apartment, and leaving her ladies in the aisles, proceeded at once to the altar, and knelt down beside the King.

Never had Editha been so much struck by any place of worship as by this wondrous chapel, with its enormous circular columns, its covered roof and gallery. To her it scarcely seemed the work of man's hand.

Having seen the Archbishop of Canterbury at the Priory, she was familiar with his stately figure, but she never yet beheld him officiate at the altar, and she listened with deepest awe to his solemn accents.

Excited by the incense with which the atmosphere was laden, and by the melodious chants of the choir, she fell into a sort of trance, from which she did not entirely recover till the service was concluded.

While she was in this rapt state, celestial visions seemed to pass before her, and she fancied she heard seraphic voices.

XVII.

HOW SIR SIMON BURLEY, THE BARON DE GOMMEGINES, AND THE LORD MAYOR SET OUT TO SUCCOUR THE BESIEGED AT ELTHAM PALACE.

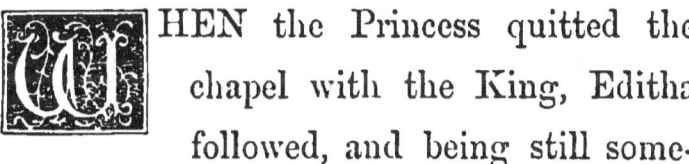HEN the Princess quitted the chapel with the King, Editha followed, and being still somewhat confused, scarcely knew where she was going, though conscious she had quitted the White Tower, and entered the palace, till she found herself in a large chamber, richly furnished, and hung with tapestry.

The King graciously saluted the Court damsels; but he bestowed such marked attention on Editha that the others were quite piqued.

But the smiles quickly fled from his Majesty's countenance, and his frivolity of manner disappeared, when he was informed by his mother of the attack upon Eltham by the rebels.

"Now, by St. George and St. Mark, this passeth all endurance!" he cried, fiercely. "Our palace attacked by this vile rabble! Cost what it may, they shall be driven off! Bid Sir Simon Burley come to me!"

"Sir Simon is mustering a troop of knights and esquires in the court, my liege!" replied the usher. "Your Majesty can see him from the window, if it pleases you to look out."

"'Tis well," cried Richard. "He has anticipated my wishes. Ha!"

The exclamation was caused by the entrance of the Baron de Gommegines, fully armed.

Richard sprang forward to meet him.

"Thou hast made ready to succour the besieged at Eltham?" he cried.

" 'Tis true, my liege," replied the Baron; "and I am come to crave your Majesty's permission to proceed thither with Sir Simon Burley."

"Sir Simon has not asked our leave, but he hath it, and so hast thou," rejoined Richard. "I will go with you. I will lead you against these rebellious hounds! Let my horse be brought out at once! I will not stay to arm—I am impatient to be off. Farewell, madam!" he added, to his mother.

Never had Editha thought Richard looked so like a king as at that moment, and she gazed at him with admiration she had not felt before. His gesture was proud, and his eyes seemed literally to flash fire.

The Princess thought he looked like his heroic father when his breast was kindled with anger.

But though delighted with this unwonted display of spirit, she deemed it prudent to restrain him.

"My liege, you must not expose yourself to needless risk!" she said.

"I care not for the risk!" he cried, impetuously. "I will go!"

But De Gommegines ventured to oppose him.

"Her Grace is in the right, my liege," he said. "You cannot leave the Tower."

"Cannot leave!" exclaimed Richard. "Who shall hinder me?"

"I will, my liege!" said Sir Simon Burley, entering at the moment.

Clad in armour from head to heel, the old knight had a snowy plume in his helm, and a long sword attached to his girdle.

"As one of the Council of Regency," he continued, in an authoritative tone, "and responsible for your Majesty's safety, I cannot allow you to leave the Tower."

For a moment Richard looked as if he would set the old knight's authority at defiance; and Editha, who watched the scene with breathless interest, thought he would break through all the trammels imposed upon him.

But Sir Simon's firmness prevailed, and in the end the young monarch, though sorely against his will, succumbed.

"I must obey you now, Sir Simon," he cried. "But a time will shortly come——"

"My liege," interrupted the old knight, "that time will never come, unless those bound to watch over you fail in their duty. I know I shall incur your Majesty's displeasure by the step I am taking, but I cannot help it."

"What are you about to do?" demanded the King, sullenly.

"I am about to join the Lord Mayor, my liege, who, with a troop of loyal citizens, is waiting for me at the Bulwark Gate," replied Sir Simon. "We shall then make all haste we can to Eltham; and I hope soon to bring your Majesty good news."

Accompanied by the Baron de Gommegines, he then departed, leaving the King in high dudgeon.

Hoping to soothe Richard's irritation, the Princess led him to a large bay window commanding the inner ward.

Beneath the trees, then growing on the patch of greensward in front of the Lieutenant's lodgings, was drawn up a company of nobles, knights, and esquires, all glittering in complete steel, and mounted on powerful chargers, making a very goodly show.

Each of the knightly companions carried

a long lance, on the summit of which fluttered a pennon. Each esquire bore a shield, emblazoned with his lord's cognizance.

Presently, Sir Simon Burley and the Baron de Gommegines came forth, and, mounting their chargers, put themselves at the head of the splendid troop.

Trumpets were then sounded, and, animated by the martial clangour, which made the battlements ring, the knightly company rode off, lowering their lances as they passed beneath the arch of the Garden Tower.

At this sight Richard turned away in deep vexation, and, as he did so, he encountered Editha's gaze, which was anxiously fixed upon him.

He could not speak to her, but addressed his mother in words meant for the damsel's ear.

"My crown is not worth wearing if I cannot fight for it!"

"Trouble not yourself on that score, my liege," replied the Princess. "These churls are unworthy of your sword. Leave others to deal with them."

On issuing from the Bulwark Gate, Sir Simon Burley and his noble companions found the Lord Mayor, with a troop of well-mounted and well-armed citizens, waiting for them.

Sir William Walworth was cased in mail, but did not bear a lance, like the knights attendant upon Sir Simon. In lieu thereof, he had a mallet affixed to his saddle-bow, and, with his strong arm, he was well able to use the heavy weapon.

Sir Simon heartily thanked the Lord Mayor, in the King's name, for his prompt and efficient response to the summons; after which the two companies rode off together.

When they had crossed London Bridge, they set spurs to their steeds, and dashed off at a gallop along the road to Blackheath and Eltham, burning to punish the presumptuous rebels.

XVIII.

WHAT BEFEL SIR OSBERT MONTACUTE ON HIS RETURN THROUGH THE SUBTERRANEAN PASSAGE.

ON re-entering the subterranean passage, Sir Osbert Montacute and the men-at-arms with him did not light the torches, but proceeded, as noiselessly as they could, along the gloomy road, in the hope of passing the intruders unperceived.

They had gone on in this manner for some time without meeting with any interruption, when a distant sound reached the ears of Baldwin, who was marching in advance, and he called to the others, in a low tone, to stop.

"I will go on alone to reconnoitre," he whispered to Sir Osbert.

Some minutes elapsed, and as he did not return, Sir Osbert became exceedingly uneasy.

The state of suspense in which he was kept was well-nigh intolerable. Vainly did he peer into the gloom—vainly listen. He could hear nothing—see nothing.

Just as he had resolved to move on, he became aware that some one was near him, and thinking it must be the guide come back, he said, in a low voice, "Is it thou, Baldwin?"

Instead of answering, the person would have retreated, had not Sir Osbert seized him by the throat, and held him fast.

"Attempt to give the alarm, and I will kill thee!" said the knight, feeling sure he had captured a rebel. "Where are thy comrades?" he added, slightly relaxing his grasp.

"They are trying to get out of this accursed place," replied the man. "They are dispersed. Some have fallen into a pit in the darkness, and are unable to get out."

A smothered laugh arose from the men-at-arms at this satisfactory intelligence.

"But where are the rest?" demanded Sir Osbert.

"'Tis a question difficult to answer," replied the prisoner, evasively, "seeing that I know not where I am myself."

"Are they in this passage?" demanded Sir Osbert, sternly. "Thou canst tell that. Thou hadst best not trifle with me, fellow. Thy name is known to me—thou art called Liripipe."

"Certes, my name is Liripipe," replied the prisoner, surprised.

"I recollect thy voice," said Sir Osbert.

"Now mark me, Liripipe! Thou shalt go on with us. If we avoid thy comrades, I will spare thee. If we meet them, thou shalt die! Take heed—my poniard is at thy throat!"

Still keeping fast hold of the prisoner, Sir Osbert compelled him to retrace his steps; but before they had got far, a noise announced that several persons were coming quickly towards them.

"They are here!" said Liripipe. "What is to be done?"

"Bid them go back instantly," replied Sir Osbert. "Say that the enemy is at hand! Shout lustily!"

Liripipe called out as he was enjoined; whereupon the rebels immediately stopped.

"Tell them to fly, and conceal themselves, or they will certainly be captured!" whispered Sir Osbert.

Liripipe obeyed, and the sound of retreating footsteps was immediately heard.

"May I follow them?" implored the

prisoner. "By St. Babylas of Antioch, I will not betray you!"

"I have not done with thee yet," rejoined Sir Osbert, slightly pricking him with the poniard. "Keep near me."

They then moved on, though somewhat slowly; for Sir Osbert had to drag the prisoner along.

Once more footsteps were heard, but they proved to be those of a friend. Next moment Baldwin came up, and announced himself.

"I did not think I should have been able to rejoin you, Sir Osbert," he said. "The rebels got hold of me, but I managed to escape while they were retreating by a side-passage."

"Is the main passage clear?" asked the knight.

"I think so," replied Baldwin. "But the villains may return."

"Forward, then!" cried Sir Osbert. "Not a moment is to be lost!"

The party then set off at a quick pace, and soon reached the outer gate, which was unlocked by Baldwin.

In fulfilment of his promise, Sir Osbert here liberated the prisoner; but he told him if he was again captured he should assuredly be hanged.

"Say to thy comrades we will soon come in search of them," added Baldwin; "and woe betide them if they are caught!"

Liripipe scarcely heard the words, though he guessed their import, but hurried off as fast as his legs could carry him.

Having carefully fastened both gates, the party made their way to the subterranean chamber.

In another minute the trapdoor was opened for them by the guard, but not till he was satisfied they were friends.

As Sir Osbert came forth, his first inquiry was, "How goes the siege?"

"I can scarce tell, my lord," replied the guard. "The rebels have gained none of the outworks, but they still obstinately continue the attack. The archers, I hear, are under the command of a certain Conrad Basset."

"I know the man you speak of, and 'tis like enough he may be their leader," said Sir Osbert. "Where is Sir John Holland?"

"Half an hour ago he was on the north battlements, my lord, and doubtless he is there still," rejoined the guard.

"Then I will go to him at once," cried Sir Osbert. "Come with me, all of you," he added, to Baldwin and the men-at-arms.

So saying, he hurried off to the battlements, but, before he reached them, loud shouts and other noises, accompanied ever and anon by the blast of a trumpet, informed him that an assault was being made by the besiegers, and vigorously repelled by the defenders of the palace.

XIX.

HOW ELTHAM PALACE WAS VALIANTLY DEFENDED BY SIR JOHN PHILPOT.

THE attack, which had commenced, as previously related, at the precise moment of the Princess's departure from the palace, had now lasted for more than two hours, without any material advantage to the assailants.

The royal residence, as we have already explained, was capable of making a stout defence, being entirely surrounded by fortified walls, and a wide, deep moat.

The moat was crossed by two stone bridges, respectively situated on the north and south of the palace, and protected by a barbacan.

The chief attack of the assailants was directed against the north barbacan, which was guarded by a dozen archers and crossbowmen, under the command of Sir John Philpot, who had sought this post as being that of the greatest danger.

And well did the brave knight prove his skill and valour. Twice were the insurgents successfully repulsed by him, when they advanced on foot, and in great numbers, to attack the barbacan, and though he sustained some slight losses, they were nothing in comparison with the damage done by him to the foe.

Conrad Basset was made a mark by the cross-bowmen and archers on the barbacan, but he escaped without injury, owing to the vigilance of a gigantic woman, who stood by his side.

This Amazon wore a breast-plate that must have been fashioned for a strongly-built man, and in addition to a broadbladed sword, carried a large triangular shield, with which she warded off many a shaft and bolt aimed at Conrad.

While these assaults were made, the Outlaw was not idle, but gave all the support he could to his friends.

Sheltered by the wood, and without much risk to the large party of archers with him, he sent constant showers of arrows against those on the battlements.

After the unsuccessful issue of the second attack, Conrad Basset repaired to the wood, where a brief conference took place between him and the Outlaw.

Somewhat discouraged, Conrad expressed an opinion that it was useless to make a further attempt.

"We have got a most resolute and skilful opponent in Sir John Philpot," he said. "He will hold the barbacan to the last. I should not have cared for Sir John Holland, but Philpot is a very different man."

"True," replied the Outlaw, "but he is not invincible; and if you defeat him, so much greater will be the honour. Rather than the siege should be abandoned, I will lead the attack myself."

Conrad might have agreed to the proposition, though it was mortifying to his pride, but Frideswide, who had followed him into the wood, and stood at a little distance, leaning on her sword, called out, in a tone that scarcely admitted of dispute—

"Do not relinquish your post! Despite Sir John Philpot, the barbacan can easily be taken, and I will tell you how."

"Show me the way, and I will thank thee heartily," rejoined Conrad.

"This is my plan," said Frideswide.

"You want a battering-ram. I will supply you with one. Not fifty yards from this spot lies a huge beam. I noticed it as I came hither. 'Twill take a dozen men to lift it, but I will help them, if need be."

"Ha! I see!" cried Conrad, joyfully. "With this beam thou wouldst burst open the postern?"

"That is my plan," said Frideswide. "When the postern is burst open, as it will be of a surety by this simple battering-ram, who is to prevent thee from entering the barbacan? Not Sir John Philpot!"

"No, by St. Anselm, not twenty Philpots!" cried Conrad. "Thou hast devised an excellent plan. The barbacan once gained, the palace will be ours!"

"Ay, marry, will it!" said the Outlaw. "When we have crossed the bridge, and appear before the gate, Sir Eustace de Valletort will be forced to surrender. Besides the plunder to be gained, the capture of a royal palace like Eltham will be of immense service to the cause, and strike terror into the breasts of the nobles."

"Let not the final assault be delayed!" cried Conrad, who was now full of ardour and impatience. "If we triumph, it will be owing to thee," he added, to Frideswide.

She spoke no word, but her look implied, "The suggestion was made to please thee."

Another assault being resolved upon, horses were brought, and ropes fastened to the ponderous beam which was found lying in the spot indicated by Frideswide.

This done, the improvised battering-ram was dragged towards the barbacan, but kept under cover of the trees till it should be required.

Very little delay occurred — Conrad Basset, as we have just remarked, being now all impatience for a fresh assault, in which he might retrieve his past ill-success.

Again trumpets were sounded by the insurgents—again the challenge was scornfully answered by the defenders of the barbacan, and still more scornfully by those on the battlements—after which a large party of rebels, headed by Conrad Basset, who was accompanied by the Amazon, again advanced to the assault.

A thick and continuous flight of arrows from the archers in the wood tended to confuse the besieged as the assailants came on, and some of the defenders of the barbacan having disappeared, the order was given by Conrad to bring on the battering-ram.

In another minute the great beam was dragged by the horses as close as it could be to the tower, and in spite of shafts, bolts, and missiles directed against them, it was laid hold of by some twenty sturdy yeomen, and in another minute propelled with resistless force against the postern.

One blow of this tremendous engine was sufficient.

The strong oaken door, though strengthened with iron, and secured with bolts and bars, yielded, and Conrad, still attended by the faithful Frideswide, rushed into the tower, followed by as many archers as he could get in with him.

A desperate conflict now took place in the lower chamber of the barbacan.

Every inch was disputed with the assailants. More than once Sir John Philpot drove them back, killing or wounding a rebel with every blow of his trenchant sword.

Conrad would undoubtedly have fallen by his hand, but for the interposition of Frideswide. Even in that fierce struggle, the valiant knight, seeing he had to deal with a woman, forbore to strike.

At length, being left almost alone—

for nearly all the men-at-arms with him were down—Sir John was compelled to retreat.

Facing the foe to the last, he passed out at the rear of the tower by a door communicating with the bridge; but being instantly followed by Conrad, Frideswide, and a score of rebels, armed with pikes, bills, and gisarmes, he stopped, and courageously confronted the whole host.

At this critical juncture the gate of the palace was thrown open, and Sir Eustace de Valletort, Sir John Holland, the Baron de Vertain, Sir Osbert Montacute, and a dozen men-at-arms, sallied forth to the rescue.

Driven back by the fierce onset of the nobles, the rebels were immediately reinforced by great numbers of their comrades, who rushed in through the barbacan gate, and Conrad returned to the attack.

Another desperate fight then took place in the centre of the bridge. For a few minutes nothing could be heard but the clash of arms, mingled with shouts, yells, and groans. Several of the rebels were thrown over the sides of the bridge into the moat.

Little assistance could be rendered to Sir Eustace by those on the walls, because they were exposed to a continuous flight of arrows from the archers whom the Outlaw had now brought to the very verge of the moat.

Despite the superior skill of the knights, they were so greatly outnumbered by the assailants, that Sir Eustace felt it would be impossible to maintain the bridge much longer, and he was, therefore, preparing for a final effort before re-entering the palace, when the sound of a trumpet was heard in the distance.

At the same moment loud and joyous shouts arose from those on the battlements.

From their elevated position on the walls, the men-at-arms could descry a clump of spears galloping along the avenue in the direction of the palace, and they therefore called out, "A rescue! a rescue!"

XX.

HOW THE PALACE WAS DELIVERED.

GUESSING the cause of the shouts, Conrad Basset, who, up to this moment, had felt sure of victory, checked the further advance of his companions, and his dismay was increased when warning cries arose from the party stationed on the outer side of the moat.

"To horse! to horse!" vociferated the insurgent archers. "The enemy is at hand!"

"Fall back instantly, and mount your steeds!" shouted Conrad to those behind him; and the order was repeated by Frideswide.

Finding the rebels were retreating, Sir

Eustace and the knights dashed upon them, and in a marvellously short space of time the bridge was entirely cleared of the assailants.

Sir Eustace did not deem it prudent to follow up his advantage, but re-occupied the barbacan, and caused the gate to be closed.

The first aim of the rebels on quitting the bridge was to regain their horses, and this was quickly accomplished, since the animals were tied to the trees at the upper end of the avenue.

While Conrad was getting together the disorderly rout, Frideswide brought him his steed, and having already secured her own horse, lent the young man great aid in his troublesome task.

Exertions of a similar kind were made at the same time by the Outlaw, and a junction was quickly formed between the two parties.

Just before the alarm was given that a troop of lances was approaching, several persons belonging to the party whose misadventures in the subterranean passages have been recounted, reappeared.

No time was allowed them to describe their proceedings, but they were ordered by the Outlaw to mount at once, and join the battalion already drawn up in the avenue.

All necessary arrangements were made with surprising celerity; and before the knights could come up, the rebel host, slightly diminished in numbers, but still presenting a very formidable appearance, was fully prepared to receive them.

Such of the insurgents as were provided with pikes were placed in the foremost ranks of the battalion, and their leaders strenuously enjoined them to stand firm.

Close to Conrad was the faithful Frideswide, who looked as undaunted as the young chief himself.

In another moment the charge was made. At the head of the party rode Sir Simon Burley and De Gommegines, shouting their battle-cry as they couched their lances.

The shock was tremendous and resistless. Bearing down all before them, unhorsing numbers, and trampling them under foot, splintering the pikes as if they had been willow-wands, the knights divided the compact mass in twain, and scattered the rebels in every direction, so that they could not reunite.

All this was the work of a few minutes.

Luckily for themselves, the two rebel leaders avoided the shock; but they saw at once that it would be impossible to rally their terror-stricken followers, who were now flying wildly off, and trying to save themselves by plunging amid the trees on either side of the avenue.

For a few moments Conrad remained stupefied by the disastrous result of the charge; but he was at length roused by Frideswide, who remained with him.

"Seest thou not that thy brother chief is gone?" she said. "He called to thee to fly, but thou didst not heed."

"I did not hear him call," replied Conrad, bitterly. "I did not see him depart. Why has he fled?"

"Because all is lost," rejoined Frideswide. "Not a man of all the host is left to stand by thee. Fly, or thou wilt be slain by these fierce knights."

"No, I will stand my ground!" he exclaimed fiercely, but despairingly. "If I must die, I will die here."

"Thou shalt not throw away thy life thus," she cried.

And seizing the bridle of his steed, she forced him away.

Their flight was perceived, and three knights instantly started in pursuit.

But both Conrad and his companion were well mounted, and the instinct of self-preservation having resumed its sway over the young man, he yielded to Frideswide's suggestion, and made for the forest lying between Eltham and Dartford.

This shelter gained, they were safe from pursuit.

"Nothing more is to be done here," said Conrad. "I will rejoin Wat Tyler at Rochester."

"Be it so," replied the submissive Frideswide.

Thus was the beleaguered palace of Eltham delivered.

Though the majority of the rebels escaped and found their way back to Rochester, numbers were slain. No prisoners were made.

The knights slew all who fell into their hands.

When the good news was brought them of the defeat of the rebels, the King and his mother were greatly rejoiced.

A banquet was given that evening at the royal palace at the Tower, at which Sir Simon Burley, the Baron de Gommegines, the Lord Mayor, and other nobles and knights assisted.

END OF BOOK THE SECOND.

BOOK III.

BLACKHEATH.

I.

THE SIEGE OF ROCHESTER CASTLE.

WHILE the events just recounted took place, Rochester Castle was besieged by the main body of the rebels, who were supplied by the townspeople with scaling-ladders, battering-rams, and mangonels, the latter being an extremely powerful engine, used at the time, for hurling large stones against the walls or gates of a fortress.

Many of the townspeople likewise assisted in the assault, which was begun without delay; and though justly accounted one of the strongest in the kingdom, it seemed unlikely the castle could long hold out against such a multitude of assailants.

Other circumstances warranted this conclusion. Not only was the fortress insufficiently garrisoned, but the Constable, Sir John de Newtoun, had reason to doubt the fidelity of his men.

Thinking to intimidate the rest, and prevent any acts of insubordination or treachery, he not only hanged Thurstan, the burgher of Gravesend, who had been sent to him by Sir Simon Burley, and whom the rebels had sworn to release, but five archers suspected of sedition, and suspended the bodies from the lofty towers of the keep, in sight of the enemy.

But the Constable's severity produced the contrary effect to that intended. It heightened the spirit of mutiny, instead of quelling it, and caused the insurgents to redouble their efforts to take the place.

Hence a siege that might have endured for months, lasted only a couple of days.

On the first assault scaling-ladders of immense length were affixed to the great partition-wall of the castle, and party after party of assailants mounted them, but were unable to gain the battlements.

Huge stones were thrown, with prodigious force, against the gates from the mangonels, and battering-rams, each worked by a score of stalwart individuals, were employed; but no entrance could be effected, and, after hours of fruitless labour, attended by great loss, the insurgents were compelled to retire.

During the night some secret communication must have taken place between the seditious garrison and the rebels; for, next morning, the latter, instead of preparing to renew the assault, made ready to enter the fortress in triumph.

The royal standard, which had hitherto floated proudly on the summit of the keep, was taken down, and replaced by a white flag. The drawbridge was lowered, and the gates thrown wide open, to admit the insurgents, who marched in, headed by Wat Tyler, fully armed, and mounted on a powerful steed.

On entering the base-court they found Sir John de Newtoun a prisoner, and guarded by a party of his own men-at-arms.

Eyeing Wat Tyler fiercely, he said to him, " Base varlet, thou hast won the castle by treachery. Never would I have surrendered it to thee."

" Go to, proud knight," rejoined Wat. " Thou hast learnt, to thy cost, that the strongest fortress cannot resist the people, when banded together."

" No fortress is safe when garrisoned by traitors," said the Constable, scornfully.

" I will not parley with thee!" cried

Wat. "Richly dost thou deserve death at our hands for thy misdeeds and cruelty. Yet are we willing to spare thy life, if thou wilt join us."

"Join you!" cried the Constable. "Darest thou make such a proposition to me, vile churl? Dost think I would dishonour myself by joining such a company of false traitors and knaves as thee and thy fellows? Undeceive thyself. Give me my sword; and then come on, all of you, and put me to death, if you can!"

"We have not done with thee yet," rejoined Wat Tyler. "Whether thou wilt join the league or not, thou shalt go with me. I have certain propositions to make to the King, and thou shalt act as my ambassador."

"Dost thou expect me to bring back his Majesty's answer to thee?" demanded the Constable.

"Assuredly," replied Wat; "and thou must pledge thy word to return."

After a moment's reflection Sir John de Newtoun said, "I will do as you desire, provided you will forthwith liberate my wife and children."

"I cannot liberate them now," said Wat Tyler. "I shall hold them as hostages for the due fulfilment of thy promise. When thou dost bring back the King's answer, whether it be favourable or otherwise, I will set them free."

"Enough!" said the Constable. "I will do thy bidding."

At a sign from Wat Tyler, he was then removed by the guard, and placed in a strong room.

The rebel leader then dismounted, and, attended by Hothbrand and several others, proceeded to the Baron's Hall, a noble chamber, which, with its three massive columns and grand arches, presented a fine specimen of Norman architecture.

Within this magnificent hall, where the Constable had dined daily during his long tenure of the post, and where he had constantly entertained nobles and knights, a banquet was spread for the rebel leader and his companions.

Before partaking of it, however, Wat Tyler descended to a large, gloomy dungeon, situated immediately beneath the Baron's Hall, wherein several State prisoners were confined, and liberated them.

He also caused all the other captives immured in the great tower to be set free.

He then returned to the banquet; and while he and his companions feasted, the castle was plundered by the insurgents and the townspeople.

Two hours afterwards, the rebel army, now enormously augmented, quitted Rochester, and commenced its march towards London.

By Wat Tyler's express command, Sir John de Newtoun was furnished with a charger, and not even guarded, since he had pledged his word not to attempt escape; but of course he was deprived of his arms.

Throughout the march he maintained a haughty deportment, and refused to converse with his captors.

Slow progress was made by the insurgents. They stopped to plunder every castle and mansion on the road, putting all who resided there to the sword, and committing other atrocious acts.

All men of law, justices, and questors, whom they caught were beheaded, by order of John Ball, who told the peasants and serfs they would never enjoy their native and true liberty till all magistrates, lawyers, and proctors were despatched.

Moreover, the crafty monk commanded them to burn and destroy all records, evidences, court-rolls, and other muniments, that their landlords might not be able to claim any right hereafter. These precautions taken, they believed themselves secure.

Many persons who would fain have avoided them, were arrested, and compelled to take the oath of fidelity to the league.

Numbers of others, likewise, flocked to the rebel standard: men in debt flying from their creditors, common robbers, sturdy beggars, outlaws, and desperadoes of all sorts.

Of such nefarious characters, whose main object was plunder, a considerable portion of the enormous host was now composed; and, as may well be supposed, it required great vigour and determination on the part of the leaders to control such an undisciplined and tumultuous army.

After a march marked by rapine and bloodshed, the vast insurgent host reached Dartford Brent, where they met the Outlaw and Conrad Basset and his men, returning from the unsuccessful siege of Eltham Palace.

Wat Tyler and John Ball were greatly enraged when they heard of the disaster, but they felt no blame could reasonably be attached to the Outlaw.

Not willing to take the overwhelming host into Dartford, Wat Tyler ordered a halt for the night on the plain; and the numerous purveyors having just returned with a plentiful supply of provisions and wine, the insurgents had no inducement to plunder the village, but were content to remain where they were.

II.

WAT TYLER REVISITS DARTFORD.

LEAVING the army to the care of the Outlaw, Hothbrand, and some of the subordinates, the rebel leader rode down into the village.

Attended by Conrad and Frideswide, and followed by a large mounted escort, among whom were Liripipe, Curthose, Grouthead, and others of the Dartford men, he rode slowly on—his banner of St. George being borne by Frideswide, and trumpets were sounded loudly as he crossed the bridge over the Brent.

At the same time the bells of the church rang joyfully, and the priests of St. Edmond's Chapel, who were alarmed for their safety, came forth, and falling on their knees before him, humbly implored his protection.

"Rest easy, good fathers," said Wat. "I have said that no one in Dartford shall be injured in person or property, and be assured I will faithfully keep my word."

Thereupon the priests, taking courage, arose and gave him their blessing.

After this momentary halt, Wat Tyler and his followers rode on, and were greeted with such feeble acclamations as could be raised by the old folks, women, and children.

Swollen with pride and success, and commanding an enormous army that implicitly obeyed all his behests, Wat Tyler had assumed a haughty, even arrogant mien, very different from his former deportment.

In fact, he scarcely looked like the same individual; and when Baldock came forth from the hostel to salute him, he was amazed by the extraordinary change in his appearance. The bewildered host made him an obeisance, as profound as he would have rendered to the highest noble.

Not displeased by the homage which he thought his due, Wat addressed the host in a condescending tone.

"Thou seest I have returned in triumph, Baldock," he said. "I have now seventy thousand brave followers on Dartford Brent —seventy thousand! What dost thou think of that? Ha!"

"I think it wonderful, my lord," replied Baldock, again bowing obsequiously. "Yet 'tis only what I expected."

"I am receiving constant accessions," pursued the rebel leader. "Before I reach London I doubt not my army will number a hundred thousand. Thus supported, the King, with whom I am about to confer, cannot refuse my demands."

"I account them already granted, my lord," rejoined Baldock.

"Mark me, Baldock," continued Wat Tyler. "A week hence there will be no council—no chancellor—no treasurer—no hierarchy—no nobles—no knights! The Commonalty of England will be supreme!"

"And you will govern the Commonalty, my lord?" observed Baldock. "Of necessity you must exercise almost sovereign sway, since the King is yet too young to rule."

"Truly, Richard will need a counsellor, like myself, to attend to the welfare of the people," said Wat. "Whatever power I possess will be exerted in behalf of the inhabitants of Dartford. Fare thee well, good Baldock; I am now about to pay a visit to the Prioress."

"A word ere you depart, my lord," remarked the host, with some hesitation. "You are aware that your dame is now staying at the Priory? You may not care to meet her?"

"Nay; I must needs see her," said Wat, knitting his brows; "though it will be for the last time!"

As he passed the green, he threw a glance at the smithy, and at the cottage adjoining it. Both places were deserted.

While looking at them, he thought of former days; but the recollection was not pleasant.

Heretofore Wat Tyler had never entered the court of the Priory, save on foot, and alone. Now, his followers filled the place.

At his loud and peremptory summons, Sister Eudoxia came to the portal, looking dreadfully frightened.

"Be not alarmed, good sister," he said. "Neither the Lady Superior nor any of the nuns shall be molested. None of my followers shall enter the Priory. But I desire to speak with the Lady Isabel."

"I cannot admit thee till I have consulted our holy mother," replied Sister Eudoxia.

She then disappeared; but presently returned, saying that the Prioress would grant him an interview.

Chancing to notice Frideswide at the same time, Sister Eudoxia added, "If that is a woman, she may enter with thee."

Thereupon Wat Tyler and Frideswide dismounted, leaving their horses with Conrad, and the Amazon was taken to the refectory by some of the nuns, who were struck with wonder at her gigantic stature; while the rebel leader was conducted to the locutory, where were the Lady Isabel and his wife.

The Prioress was seated in the large oak chair when he entered, and, being greatly offended by his haughty deportment and overweening manner, did not rise to receive him.

He scarcely noticed his wife, who gazed at him in astonishment, not unmingled with anger.

"Holy mother, you have doubtless heard of the great success of the insurrection?" he said.

"I have heard that the rebels under thy command have done much mischief, and plundered many religious houses," rejoined the Prioress, coldly. "Thou art bound in gratitude to respect this convent."

"I mean to respect it," said Wat. "I am come to speak to you, holy mother, respecting Editha. I mean to take her with me."

"Take her with thee?" exclaimed his wife. "I would never consent to such a step. Luckily, thou canst not execute thy wicked design. Editha has left the convent, and is now under the care of the Princess."

"Under the care of the Princess!" cried Wat, with a look of disappointment and vexation. "Thou didst wrong to part with her without my consent—which would have been refused," he added to the Prioress. "I had other designs for her."

"What designs?" demanded the Lady Isabel, uneasily.

"I meant to make her Queen of England!" rejoined Wat.

"Hold thy peace!" cried his wife. "Thou art mad to talk thus."

"Nay; by my troth!" rejoined Wat. "'Tis no visionary scheme, as you shall find. I will take her from the Princess, and force the young King to wed her!"

"And thinkst thou, presumptuous man, that such an alliance will be permitted?" remarked the Prioress. "I tell thee no!"

"And I say 'Yea!'" cried Wat, in a tone of thunder that made his listeners tremble.

"My word is now law, and I will have it so. My daughter shall be wedded to the King!"

"Thy daughter!" exclaimed the Lady Isabel, indignantly.

Then checking herself suddenly, she added, "Thou wilt not sacrifice her thus! Were thy insane scheme carried out 'it would be fatal to her!"

"Ay, truly would it," said Dame Tyler. "The King would repudiate her."

"Not while I am what I am!" rejoined the rebel leader, sternly.

"Thy pride will bring thee to destruction, thou headstrong and mistaken man!" said the Prioress, in a tone of severe rebuke. "As thou wouldst live hereafter, I charge thee not to meddle with Editha."

"I am not to be turned from my fixed purpose," he rejoined. "All I have hitherto attempted has succeeded, and this will not fail. I shall wed my daughter to the King."

Disregarding his wife's prayers and entreaties, and the Prioress's expressions of anger, he quitted the locutory, and strode along the corridor to the porch.

Frideswide went forth at the same time with him.

Just as he was about to mount his steed, his wife rushed out, exclaiming, distractedly—

"Wouldst cast me off, Wat? wouldst cast me off?"

"Begone! thou art unsuited to me, woman!" he rejoined, harshly.

"Unsuited or not, I will go with thee!" she rejoined, trying to cling to him.

But Frideswide thrust her back; and Wat Tyler, without bestowing another look upon the unhappy woman, rode off, and, followed by his attendants, returned at once to Dartford Brent.

III.

THE HERMIT'S WARNING.

 SUMPTUOUS tent, part of the plunder of Rochester Castle, was pitched for Wat Tyler in the centre of the plain; but, though fatigued, he felt little inclination for slumber, and after disencumbering himself of the heaviest portion of his armour, and placing his sword by his side, he merely threw himself on the couch.

A lamp, hanging from the top, illumined the interior of the tent.

It might be about two hours after midnight when Wat, who had sunk into a troubled doze, was roused by a noise outside; and as he started up and seized his sword, the folds of the tent were drawn back, and Frideswide, fully armed, stood before him.

"What brings thee here at this hour?" demanded the rebel leader.

"First, learn that thy drunken sentinels are worse than nought, being both fast asleep," she rejoined. "I spurned them with my foot, but could not wake them. A traitor might have slain thee sleeping, had he chosen."

"To thy business," said Wat.

"There is a holy hermit without, who would fain speak with thee. He calls himself Friar Gawen. I discovered him moving, like a spectre, among the slumbering host; and, finding he was seeking thy tent, I brought him hither."

"Admit him. I know the holy man."

Next moment, the hermit, who was waiting outside the tent, was introduced.

As he entered, he threw back his cowl.

His conductress would have withdrawn, but Wat Tyler bade her remain.

"I would speak to thee alone, my son," said the friar.

"It cannot be, holy brother," replied Wat. "Heed not the presence of this courageous damsel. She can keep a secret as well as a man."

"Better," observed Frideswide.

"Thou hearest. Say on."

"Then blame me not if I offend thee," replied the hermit. "I have had a vision in my cell, and thy fate has been revealed to me."

"My fate!" exclaimed Wat.

"Art thou prepared to hear it?" demanded the hermit, solemnly.

"Yea," replied the rebel leader. "I shrink not from the knowledge."

"Then learn that, before another week, thou wilt die a bloody death!"

A chill, as of the grave, fell upon Wat, and seemed to benumb his faculties.

For nearly a minute he scarcely drew breath, but remained staring fixedly at the hermit.

Seeing the effect produced, Frideswide stepped up, and shook him roughly.

"Be thyself!" she cried. "Be not troubled by the foolish talk of this visionary friar! I would not have brought him to thee had I guessed his errand. Shall I take him hence?"

"Listen to me ere thou dost dismiss me," said the hermit. "Quit this rebellious host before daybreak, and thy life may yet be spared."

"Wilt thou do that?" cried Frideswide, to the rebel leader. "Thou art not what I deem thee if thou wilt. Thou hast an army, with which thou canst exterminate all the nobles of the land, and raise thee up a sovereignty an thou choosest. Wilt thou abandon it at the word of a drivelling friar?"

"No!" cried Wat Tyler, springing to his feet, and glaring fiercely at the hermit. "I see through thy design, false priest! Thou art sent to fright me back by idle warnings. I laugh at them. I will march on courageously as ever. Nor will I pause till I have reached the mark at which I aim."

"March on, then, proud man, and meet thy doom," said the hermit. "I have warned thee."

And he turned to depart.

"Stay!" cried Wat. "Confess thou wert sent to me by the Prioress of St. Mary."

"I was sent to thee by thy deserted

wife, to whom I related the vision," replied the hermit.

"I guessed as much," said Wat. "Begone!"

"Shall he be allowed to go free?" asked Frideswide.

"Ay; and do thou convey him to the outskirts of the camp," replied Wat. "I would not harm should come to him."

Friar Gawen fixed an earnest, imploring look on the rebel leader; but seeing no change in his looks, he quitted the tent with Frideswide.

About half an hour afterwards, Wat Tyler, having put on his armour, and girded on his sword, went forth.

The sentinels were still sleeping at the door of the tent; but he did not disturb them.

IV.

THE OUTLAW ACCEPTS THE COMMAND OF THE ESSEX BATTALION.

IT must be borne in mind that the season when the march of the rebels took place, was not far from midsummer, when the nights are shortest, and ordinarily so fine and warm, that there can be no great hardship in sleeping upon a heath without other cover than the sky.

By the grey light of earliest dawn, which gave additional effect to the extraordinary picture presented to him, Wat Tyler beheld thousands upon thousands of peasants lying stretched upon the ground in every direction, almost the whole of the countless host being still buried in slumber.

Some few were astir, and here and there a watch-fire was blazing, the yellow flame contrasting with the grey glimmer of dawn; but the general appearance of the plain was that of an immense battle-field, thickly strewn with corpses of the slain.

This idea occurred to Wat as he gazed around, and filled him for a time with sombre presentiments.

Not having altogether shaken off the effect of the hermit's warning, he could not repress the dread thought that ere a single week had passed that enormous host might be scattered and destroyed, and he himself, their haughty leader, gone.

Occupied by such reflections, he almost insensibly quitted the camp, and was walking slowly on, when he heard a shout behind him, and turning, perceived the

Outlaw galloping towards him, accompanied by two other persons on horseback, whom he did not recognise.

Seeing his brother chief was in quest of him, he immediately stopped, and next moment the Outlaw and his companions came up.

"I have been to thy tent," said Jack Straw, "and not finding thee there, have come in quest of thee. A message has just been brought to me by our friends here, Rochford and Thurrock," he continued, pointing to the two individuals with him, "to the effect that ten thousand trusty Essex men are ready and eager to join us, but are unable to cross the river."

" 'Tis true," said Rochford.

" Since they cannot come to us, I will go to them," pursued Jack Straw, "and put myself at their head. How say you, brother? Have I determined aright?"

"Ay, marry," replied Wat Tyler. "You will bring the battalion round to the north side of London. We shall thus completely environ the city."

"Such is my design," said the Outlaw; "and I had already imparted it to our friends here."

Rochford and Thurrock bowed, and the latter said, "The vessel in which we crossed awaits us in Dartford Creek. Our confederates are stationed near Barking."

"My chief concern is that I cannot capture Eltham Palace," observed the Outlaw.

"The Palace will fall into our hands hereafter," said Wat. "I shall not waste time in beseiging it now."

"Then all is settled," cried Jack Straw. "To-morrow morn, if all goes well, I shall have brought my battalion to Hampstead Heath, and shall fix my tent on the highest point of the hill, whence I can survey London, which will shortly be in our power. Farewell!"

So saying, he galloped off with his companions, and dashing down the sloping sides of the hill, proceeded to the creek, where they embarked with their horses in the vessel waiting for them, and crossed the Thames to Purfleet.

END OF VOL. II.